FROM BAMBOO TO MANGO

COVER PHOTOS

Front panel *(top)—Triplets delivered at Luho, China, hospital/ Moving day for camping in India/ Charles in China, 1906/ (lower)—Dr. George DeVol, right, Catherine's father, with his brother Charles/ (lower right)—Catherine and Charles DeVol as students at Marion College in Indiana.*

Back panel *(clockwise, beginning lower left)—Catherine and Everett Cattell with their daughter Barbara Brantingham and grandchildren Jeannie and David (back row), and Jonathan and Timothy (front), Taiwan, 1974/ "Auntie" Margaret Holme/ Barbara, Mary Catherine, and David Cattell with their pets at Chhatarpur/ Charles and Catherine visiting at the Quakerage, Nanking, China/ In an Indian village around the campfire.*

FROM BAMBOO TO MANGO

by
Catherine D. Cattell

with foreword
by
Robert Hess

THE BARCLAY PRESS
Newberg, Oregon 97132

FROM BAMBOO TO MANGO

Library of Congress Catalog Card Number: 76-5942

PAPERBOUND EDITION: ISBN 0-913342-23-8
Published January, 1978

CLOTHBOUND EDITION: ISBN 0-913342-05-X
First printing, May 1976
Second printing, August 1977

Photographs on cover and within the book were selected from the personal family albums of Catherine DeVol Cattell. Graphic design of book, cover, and illustrations by Stan and Shirley Putman. Editing, setup, and offset printing by The Barclay Press, Newberg, Oregon, United States of America.

Contents

Illustrations

The Author

CATHERINE CATTELL is the daughter of Drs. George and Isabella DeVol, who were medical doctors in the Friends China Mission. She was born in China and spent her early life there, attending school in China and later in Ohio, graduating from Ashley High School and from Marion College, Marion, Indiana.

She and her husband were in pastorates in Ohio prior to their going to India in 1936. Mrs. Cattell worked in the villages of India, especially with the women. She is author of the book, *Till Break of Day*, a volume of sketches of Indian life. During their last year in India she completed another book to teach illiterate Indian villagers the gospel message by flannelgraph.

After their return to the United States, Everett Cattell served as superintendent of Ohio Yearly Meeting (now Evangelical Friends Church—Eastern Region) and later as president of Malone College in Canton, Ohio. They now live in Columbus, Ohio, where they continue their service in speaking, preaching, and writing.

Foreword

Catherine Cattell introduced many of us to the anxieties and aspirations of the villagers of Central India in her book, *Till Break of Day*. We heard the villagers speaking to us and, in turn, we listened as she addressed the villagers with the thrilling message of hope. *From Bamboo to Mango* is a fascinating account of her experiences as a child of Quaker medical missionaries . . . reared in China . . . married in the United States . . . a missionary with her husband Everett in India . . . and mother of missionaries now serving in Taiwan. She admits she is never quite sure whether to be Asian or American in viewing life.

These stories are set over a wide period of time, spanning three generations. The events and locale have on them the imprint of the particular time in which they occurred and yet are timeless as they capture the laughter and pathos of sensitive children. She traces the development and variation of certain Christian convictions over a period of years, but there is a deep-rooted dedication to biblical principles. There are humorous descriptions of eccentricities found among the missionaries and their supporters, but one never doubts her loyalty to Christian missions.

Some of the experiences in this interesting autobiography win our attention because in them we relive our own childhood. This interest is measurably deepened, however, when we travel with her in mainland China, India, and on Taiwan. No less absorbing are the descriptions of adjustment in complex America for one who has been reared in conservative Asia.

Absent from these descriptions are the drone of the travelogue or the singsong of dialogue. Rather, travel and discussion meet us in lively stories and witty descriptions of characters who influenced the lives of each generation of this missionary family.

Some of us have had the privilege of hearing Catherine Cattell tell these stories around the table or by the fireside. The value of this book is that we hear her tell the stories, now, with the same enthusiasm and contagion. One can see missions clearly and feel the moving of the Spirit in a missionary family while reading this book.

—Robert Hess

Preface

From Bamboo to Mango is a very personal story—not of my life or of mission work in China or India. It is rather the reactions of a missionary child born and brought up in the Orient, of her adjustment to America, and of her reactions to life as a missionary mother.

There are so many ways of reacting to life, particularly to the special stresses that life in a foreign country puts upon one, especially upon children of missionaries. Many of our contemporaries of China days have themselves become missionaries. Some are well-known names in the diplomatic corps, well adjusted as world citizens, prizing opportunities provided by travel and exposure to other cultures, and acquaintance with people of great vision and courage.

There are, however, others who have reacted negatively—some in actual rebellion, and some reacting in sophisticated ways, as for instance the late Pearl Buck, who was a contemporary of our Nanking days.

Many have felt deprived and fragmented and resent sacrifices required of missionaries, especially the frequent separations from parents.

There are still others who love the country, the people, and the culture of their childhood and never feel really comfortable in America nor adjust to life among relatives, or to American schools.

At Malone College, where my husband served as president for twelve years after our return to America, I saw once more children of missionaries struggling with their adjustments and taking various ways. Being an MK (missionaries' kid) myself, and mother of three, and now a grandmother of four, I have had a special concern for transplanted children.

In the light of all this, I felt a desire to share in a very personal way my own reactions to life.

I am deeply grateful that the privilege was mine of knowing the pioneer missionaries in both China and India. They have given me proof, when I had none of my own, of answered prayer, of faith becoming sight. I delighted in their idiosyncrasies. They made strong, courageous people seem so human and lovable. I loved them all dearly. Their letters are still in my file and they continue to lift me. I wanted to be like them.

As a child, I often felt lonely, homesick maybe, but never neglected or deprived. I loved China as a child, India as an adult, and since I have spent half my life in the Orient, I have also had very difficult adjustments to make in America. There have been dark days, sorrows and troubles, frustrations and heartache, but I have found God faithful not only to pioneer missionaries but to me and mine, and if I had another life to live, I would want to be available for God to call wherever He would choose. These experiences of the past have had a profound effect upon me, making me what I am and, in a sense, what my children and my children's children are too.

A bamboo never becomes a mango tree. Each keeps its own identity though found in many places around the world. Each may, however, do better rooted in its own native soil. An American never really becomes an Oriental.

But, with Christians, the will of God is the native soil. The whole world is His and He provides nourishment, strength, and security wherever He may choose to plant us.

Acknowledgments

THE MANUSCRIPT OF *From Bamboo to Mango* would never have seen the light of day had I not had the help and encouragement of many people.

First of all, my brothers have read the manuscript for accuracy, as also have our daughters, and I am grateful to them for allowing me to share the intimate details of their lives.

I availed myself of the professional help of Dr. Robert Lair, head of the English Department of Malone College, who went through with a "fine comb" looking into grammar and giving advice on many matters. For his help I am deeply grateful.

Helen King also made some excellent suggestions. She has had years of experience editing manuscripts, and I was grateful for her encouragement.

Thelma Wakeman typed and retyped patiently and was always ready to do it again. Bless her!

Agnes Tish, president of the Evangelical Friends Alliance Women's Missionary Union, introduced the manuscript to Barclay Press. I am most grateful to her, and to Barclay Press for accepting it for publication. I am also grateful to Harlow Ankeny and the review committee of Barclay Press (Phyllis Cammack, Margaret Lemmons, Earl P. Barker, and Hazel Pierson) for the hours of reading and helping to put it together in its present form. The distance between Ohio and Oregon has made it necessary for them to take the burden of putting on the final touches. Phyllis Cammack and Rachel Hinshaw performed the final editorial functions of editing and organization of illustrations with Stan Putman designing the 28 pages of illustrations, the jacket, and chapter headings.

Many times I have put the writing aside feeling I could never have the courage to write so openly about our family for others to see, but there have been those who kept it alive and insisted on my finishing it. Of these, Anna Nixon, a fellow missionary and favorite "auntie" of the India staff, is one. Paul Langdon, a long-time friend of the DeVol family, is another, and most of all my dear husband Everett, who kept buying paper and insisted that I "write it all up."

And so, I thank one and all, for this has indeed been a joint project.

—*Catherine DeVol Cattell*

Dedicated to
My Children
and
My Children's Children

Section I
Bamboo

Chapter 1
West Gate

Chapter 2
Mountain Stream

Chapter 3
Pet Snake and Sudden Storm

Chapter 4
Roots in the Attic

Chapter 5
Camphor Tree

Chapter 6
"Distress on Horseback"

Chapter 7
A Grey Blanket over the Valley

Chapter 8
Farewell, Bamboo

The Bamboo Tree

STRAIGHT AND TALL and dainty is the bamboo. It casts a delicate lacy pattern on the ground below as the sun filters through its slender, pointed leaves. A bamboo grove is a place where monks walk in quiet meditation, and just as suitable for a picnic.

The bamboo has hundreds of uses. It becomes a scaffold for building. It is hollow and becomes a pipe to carry water from the spring in the mountain to the village far away. It is used to irrigate the farmland and rice fields.

From the moment a shoot peeps out of the ground, it is food—a delicious vegetable that gives character to every dish in which it is used.

Bamboo may be cut in small slivers for toothpicks or even chopsticks with which to eat rice, bean sprouts, or bamboo shoots. It may be a pole placed over a man's shoulder to carry water, night soil, or baskets of vegetables on each end.

Much of Chinese art uses the bamboo: in painting, in jade, patterns on china dishes, carvings, and ivory, brass, and woven into the lovely brocade cloth that becomes handsome garments.

It may be a chair, or a cane, or a screen.

Bamboo serves humanity in such a variety of ways.

I like best to think of it as a channel for water to flow through to reach the dry places where water is needed—the brown places that should be green. It is a hollow wood, empty of itself and easily made into a very effective channel of blessing.

Strength and beauty combine to serve the needs of a great people. It is indispensable.

Bamboo speaks to me of China.

Chapter 1
West Gate

Luho, a walled city in Central China, had seven gates opening out to the countryside each morning at daybreak and closing to the outside world each night at sunset. There were watchmen at the gates to supervise the comings and goings and to keep an eye on travelers who visited their city.

These same gates closed against new and foreign influences so that life, as I knew it in Luho, was much as it had been for centuries except that two American doctors had entered those gates to live and practice medicine. One of these doctors was my father; the other was my mother. There was neither a home nor a hospital when they first came—just the city itself, to which they brought faith and courage to start at the beginning.

At West Gate Father was able to obtain land, and the building for a hospital and for a home across the street was begun.

The city itself had a grey look about it. The city walls were of grey brick, as were the houses along the street, joined each to the other in one continuous line on both sides. The roofs were of black tile. The streets, too narrow to let in much sunlight, were grey with shadow and smoke, and the large grey slabs of stone that paved the street were rutted by centuries of wheelbarrow tracks and polished by the tread of many feet. They were crowded with human life pushing a path through the rest of humanity, crowding it into open stores at each side, having to make room as well for donkeys, wheelbarrows, and water carriers.

Now and then there was a sedan chair in which some dignitary who did not wish to mingle so rudely with the jostling crowd was able to travel unruffled. Or it might be the wife of an official whose bound feet, as well as her high position, made walking an impossibility. Whatever the occasion, the coolies who carried the chair shouted to all passersby, "Make way," "Get out of the way," along the whole length of the journey; and people and animals herded together on both sides to let them pass.

Supplies to meet the needs of the city had to be carried in through the city gates from the surrounding countryside or from river junks transporting them from other parts of China. Coolies then unloaded them on the banks and carried them great distances to the stores and shops throughout the city. There were bolts of grass linen, blue cotton, cloth, sacks of rice, tins of tea, farm produce, five-gallon tins of kerosene, and even the water to drink from the river itself, swinging wildly from each end of a bamboo pole balanced from a man's shoulder. Night soil, the waste from all the houses, had also to be carried out to the reservoirs provided for it so that it could be used as fertilizer.

The streets were always wet from the spillings of all kinds of water: hot water to the homes for baths from the hot-water store; hot, cold, dirty, or foul smelling, it all had to come and go, sloshing and spilling, carried by men to the rhythm of "ai ya ho, ai ya ho," which was a little tune intended to keep the water carriers more in rhythm along the city streets.

Pedestrians watched for puddles and slippery places while they were shoved along, dodging and coping as best they could with the noise and smells and clamor. Had there been beauty, there would have been small chance of seeing it, as it took all one's faculties to watch the next step. The streets were not the tree-lined of China's big cities. They were for business, and the business was to move humanity along its narrow lengths as rapidly as hurrying feet, wheelbarrows, and donkey trains could be made to move.

The streets of Luho were full of excitement and tempting odors, as well as foul ones, because of the open restaurants and tea houses along the way offering a wide choice of irresistible rice cakes called *bao tzes* (steaming hot buns with a ball of meat inside) or *jao dzes* (meat and vegetable in boiled dumpling)—in the exact moment of doneness.

There was cotton candy spun to the finest thread and sesame seed candy. There were odors of hot peanut oil, the smoke of incense from a thousand homes, and raw fish at the fish market, and there was the ever-penetrating odor of donkeys. There was the musty smell of cloth shops. There was the fragrance of jasmine and the tangy odor of spice and the over-sweet of dried dates. All these smells—fair and foul—mingled together to make up the odor of a Chinese street. There was nothing strange about all this to Charles and me. Luho was our hometown.

Charles was a redhead, and the Chinese do not have red-headed children EVER. My hair was black, which was very convenient, as black hair made more sense to our Chinese neighbors. Hence, I was called only a foreign devil, but my brother had the distinction of being called a redheaded foreign devil. I hated being called a devil, but to be a redheaded devil was really a bit unsettling.

Charles was only older by two and a half years, and we did everything together; or, more accurately, I did everything just a few steps behind him. If he walked on stilts, so did I, between tumbles; if he chased butterflies, I was right behind with the jar. Whatever Charlie collected, I hunted for him, and when he mounted birds, I held the wings and legs while he made a nice straight incision down the abdomen just like Papa did at the hospital!

The only other foreigner in the city was Auntie Holme, a single lady who lived at East Gate and at the opposite end of the street. There was a girls' school at that end and the Christian church, where an American bell rang out the times of service. Sometimes Auntie Holme had guests, sometimes a companion, another "auntie" temporarily, but Auntie Holme was permanent and became permanently a part of our family. (Was there ever a missionary woman on the field that was not an "auntie" to all the children in the mission? I think it unlikely.)

The family, in my mind, was never confined to the group of missionaries. The Chinese were the larger part of my world, and I was with them a greater part of the time. We children felt perfectly at home among them, running in and out of their homes, particularly of those homes that were in the same compound. When we were with them, we ate, sat, spoke, and behaved as they did. In our own home, we were American children. It was as though there were two of each of us, for both worlds, both cultures, both languages were ours; and we bridged the difference by being whatever was required at the moment. Our family included both Chinese and what we called ourselves, "foreigners."

The West Gate compound was enclosed by a rectangular grey brick wall. Our house was a two-storied grey box with two rooms on each floor and an upstairs verandah along one side, from which we could see all the excitement of Chinese life. We gazed down upon it and longed to be a part, but our gate was kept locked by Lao Shih (Old Tenth), who had the key and whose main job as gatekeeper was to keep us inside and intruders outside. He also tended the garden and fed the chickens, ducks, goats, dogs, and the donkey, which he would lead around when we wanted to ride.

Father kept us supplied with pets, and when he brought the sad-faced donkey to live in our compound, our joy knew no bounds! No name fit him quite so well as Eeyore of Winnie-the-Pooh fame. He was never a happy animal, and being totally unaccustomed to lively American children, he kicked back at times, even kicking me off his back and breaking my only doll, Lao Shih's efforts notwithstanding.

Lao Shih had a wife, but she was strictly his family and not ours! She lived at the gatehouse with only Lao Shih to supervise her comings and goings, and we were never a part.

But next door to Lao Shih lived Tsi Si Fu hard against the gatehouse on one side and the front compound wall on another. He lived there with his wife Tsi Sao Dzi. She was his cook and he was ours. Mother had trained him well, and he had a flair for it of his own. His layer cakes were famous for looks as well as for taste, filled with custard cream pudding between the layers and sugared nuts on top.

No one cooked eggs like Tsi Si Fu. They were masterpieces of culinary art. We sometimes had beaten egg whites piled on toast with the yolk done just enough, lying unbroken, baked in the nest of golden fluff.

Mother knew about foods, and Tsi Si Fu was a willing learner. We made our own coffee from bran and molasses, and everything was made from the basic kind of scratch that America has not seen in a long time. The kitchen was the cook's workshop, set out a little from the house but joined by a covered passageway.

The cook and his wife did the work of the house—he the cooking and dishwashing, marketing, and table setting; she the beds and cleaning. She did the washing and he the ironing. Now and then we helped her, never him, and we learned to work her way. Tsi Si Fu sprinkled the clothes in the most delightful manner. He filled his mouth with water and then by moving his lips was able to put a fine spray wherever he wanted to. We practiced this but never mastered the secret of an even spray. It turned out to be more like spitting on the clothes.

It was not in our house that we had the most fun helping. It was with the cook's wife in her kitchen, where she made Chinese food for Tsi Si Fu and herself. She had a high brick stove, whitewashed, with two round holes in the top, fitted with round-bottomed iron kettles. The fire was fed slowly from behind with *luchai* (tall marsh grass), which burned in a flash so that it had to be tended steadily. This I loved to do, and although it was "officially" forbidden to eat at the cook's house, it never seemed very wrong to just taste the food. Certainly it was most delicious.

Meals at our house were the happiest times of day, particularly breakfast. Perhaps it was because Father and Mother were always there and our days began with togetherness and time for talk. We ate millet, and sometimes broom corn or puffed rice in season, for it was a special part of New Year's celebration and the rice was puffed in the street before our eyes.

It was, however, not so much the food as Father that made breakfast so special. He taught us something every morning. He was the eternal teacher. One day it was prisms; another day it was the law of gravity. One day he drew us a picture of the eye and kept us at the table until we had learned the names of all its parts.

Another day Father suddenly became aware of the fact that I was eight years old and had never learned the bones of the body! What negligence on his part! So we set out to learn all 208 of them. I learned not to say, "I don't know what to do." Father could always think of something. That's how I read *Ben Hur* at the age of nine!

At night, after supper, it was Mother's time. She was all ours for those going-to-bed moments. She read us stories from a book called *Line upon Line.* She read Bible stories and then told us one without names, expecting us to identify it. She read us about Brer Rabbit and Brer Fox and many nature stories.

Father was something of a poet, and he rhymed a prayer for us. Mother taught it to us in stages, and we learned to say it faster and faster as the prayer became more familiar.

Our Father in heaven,
We thank Thee tonight
For food and for clothing
For health and for sight.

Whatever of evil
This day I have done
Forgive me, dear Father,
Through Jesus Thy Son.

And help me to live
Well pleasing to Thee
Now and forever
Thy dear child to be.

Bless Father and Mother
And all dear to me
The sick and the hungry
And all dear to Thee.

Mother told us about her girlhood in America—it seemed as good as fairy tales and about as possible. America was a name to us, like Utopia. Where was it and what was it like? We could not say, but it sounded wonderful, and Mother loved it and often showed us pictures of her family there. The world around us, however, was a Chinese world, and since we had no experience of her world, it was like showing pictures of heaven.

Every Sunday we went to church at East Gate, where Auntie Holme lived. Father was the pastor of the church, but Auntie Holme was also a powerful preacher and at times she preached. More often she played the organ, and I sat beside her on the front seat on the women's side while Mother ushered the ladies to their seats and helped them find their place in the hymnbook or Bible, both of which were provided upon arrival. There was a divider down the middle of the church, and the men and boys sat on the other side.

The old ladies loved to sing. I remember some dear souls, slower to find the page, would start at the beginning when they found it no matter where Auntie Holme had gotten in her leading. Occasionally, they wound up with their own private solos (because they didn't want to miss any of the good words) with Mrs. Hu's falsetto voice putting a little off-key flourish at the very end.

Singing in unison came slowly, but it came, they tell me. In my day, however, Mother rushed from one to another hurrying the process of finding the hymn, and Auntie Holme added to her loudest organ tones her own quavery high voice to mark out the tune and time more distinctly.

Auntie Holme must have had a good voice at one time, but this leading the singing against such odds was what broke it down into the quaver. She played the offertory for the service, and I loved above all to hear the organ by itself. My highest ambition was to be just like Auntie Holme. She and I were friends, and she had a delightful way of treating me with grown-up courtesy.

I must have known that Auntie Holme was English, but her England and Mother's Ohio were equally unreal and equally fascinating. I had no idea that Auntie Holme was not really, truly family. She was a small, thin little lady with grey hair done in a knot on the top of her head. Her face was deeply lined, but the lines were happy ones, and her laugh was such fun, having the same quavery sound as her singing.

Our family ate many meals at East Gate, and she was often in our home, but hers was for some time the only other house in Luho to visit, and it was always special.

There was a certain room in the hospital that held great attraction for me. The room was locked, but now and then I was allowed to spend the morning in the room with Mother. It was the storeroom. There were yards of cloth, sheeting, bolts of gauze, and parcels of all kinds from America. Once the room was well supplied with dolls—the china head variety dressed in handmade clothing—miniatures of what women in America wore in that period. They were beautiful and had been sent out by missionary societies in America to be given out to little girl patients who had to be in the hospital a long while.

I had no doll of my own, and I was not permitted to have one of these because they had been sent for "the work." I was allowed to choose which one to give out next, and it often took me an extraordinarily long time to make up my mind! There was the day when one patient produced triplets! I held a real live baby, but there again was the problem—which one to hold. I gave out from the storeroom three blankets to the same mother in the same day!

Ming Djen was one of the patients in the women's ward that I visited every day. She was a very pretty girl with an abscessed leg. Her parents had died and she was forced to work in rice fields, often knee deep in water and mud. Abscesses were common, but hers was very serious and she stayed in the hospital for a long time. It became apparent that her life was not only one of hard work but of cruel subjection to the whims of evil men. Father legally adopted Ming Djen, and although she eventually went back to the country to live, she was married to a suitable man and was a radiantly happy young wife and mother. She came to visit us often and very respectfully spoke of my father as "*fu tsin.*"

An event took place in Luho while we were still very young that caused widespread excitement throughout the city but very particularly in our West Gate household. A new family was coming to join the Mission, Walter and Myrtle Williams and Walter R., Jr. Father had been the only man in the Mission in our short experience, with a number of "aunties," but there had never been an "uncle." But a whole family coming meant a man would join Father; that they had a baby boy was further cause for rejoicing—another boy in the Mission and not a brother!

Uncle Walter started the Friends Academy for boys, which was to play such a vital part in the work of the Mission in the changing of many lives. Village and country boys, as well as sons of officials, were given an opportunity for a fine education.

The two families became knitted together in closest fellowship. Uncle Walter, Aunt Myrtle, and Auntie Holme, with our parents, were a team, and none of us knew at the beginning how very much they were to mean to each other as the years came and went.

In 1911 the Republic of China was born, but not without war and much bloodshed. The Manchu yoke was not easily thrown off, and war came to our gates in Luho.

Mother was desperately ill with malaria. Charles and I were both burning with fever from malaria in the other bedroom.

Liu Da Ma was our amah. She did what she could, along with the cook and his wife. We were all very ill, and Father kept the hospital going as well as the family across the street. Myrtle Williams came over in the evening to bathe us and try to bring down the fever. She went from bed to bed with comfort and a cooling hand.

One day Father came rushing into the house with the word from the yamen that we must all leave the city immediately. It was an order. The Mayor did not want to be responsible for what happened to the foreigners. Mother was carried to the river bank in a stretcher, we children were put into a sedan chair, and all of us were taken by boat to Shanghai, where we were refugees for several months. The Luho and Nanking missionaries took over an entire building—our family was in one room, the Williams family in another, the single ladies on the second floor, and the orphans and Chinese dependents on the third. Father went back alone to Luho, where the hospital was used as the Red Cross headquarters and the wounded soldiers were treated.

The Manchu yoke was overthrown. Yuan Shih Kai became the first President of the Republic of China. Eventually we returned to Luho and Mother to the task of unbinding the poor broken and crippled feet of the ladies who had never known anything but the tortures of bound feet. Bound feet for women and queues for men were symbols of Manchu rule, and the new government abolished both with a stern hand.

I became acquainted with the ladies of the city and also of the nearby cities in this way, as our mother was the only doctor in the area who could salvage their tormented feet and give them back some degree of use again. The gratitude of these ladies brought them to our gate, and they came to call bearing gifts of silk embroidery and scrolls with characters of appreciation inscribed. I loved these visits, and mother let me serve the tea and watermelon seeds to all who came.

There was always something to do. Mother loved picnics, and Father occasionally hunted pheasant in the evenings, so they combined their interests, making a great excitement for us children. Tsi Si Fu packed the picnic lunch, and off we went outside the city gate to a quiet place in the country. Mother carried the food with her in the sedan chair. Charles trudged along beside Father on foot, and I got to ride the donkey with Lao Shih pulling both of us along the city streets, through the city gate to the open countryside beyond the grey city walls. We passed bamboo groves as we went along. The trees cast a lacy pattern on the ground as the afternoon sunlight filtered through their slender and pointed leaves.

Everywhere there were rice fields and the squeaking of treadmills. We could see a line of men and women walking endlessly on the bamboo steps that moved on a belt bringing the water up through bamboo pipes from the river into the thirsty rice fields.

Mother and I loved the bamboo groves, but we passed them by to the picnic spot where Father and Charles would hunt pheasants.

As the city gates closed at dark, we had to watch the time, and it seemed we were always in a bit of a hurry. On the way back, from atop the donkey, I could see Father and Charles walking together, with the pheasant hanging between them. Mother's chair was far ahead nearing the city. Alas, Lao Shih had led the donkey and me on the wrong path. There were rice fields with water knee-deep on both sides of the narrow mud path.

"Ai ya—we are on a dike between rice fields that leads nowhere," said Lao Shih to the donkey, "we have to turn you around. It is late, so hurry up." He pushed the donkey to indicate the desirability of turning to the opposite direction, but the donkey—being somewhat clumsy and dull of understanding—fell into the rice field with me on it and Lao Shih went with us, splash! into a foot or so of muddy water.

We arrived at the city gate just before it was shut for the night, but only because Lao Shih shouted ahead announcing our predicament and asking for a little extension of time. There we came: Lao Shih, soaking wet, leading the half-drowned beast down the streets of the city. I was perched on top of the beast, shivering, mud-besplattered, and wet to the skin, weeping bitterly as I rode along to the great amusement of those we met along the way. We were humiliated, but the humiliation became a bond between Old Tenth, the gatekeeper, and me. I went home to a hot bath sent in from the hot-water shop, and there were clean clothes; but his clothes were dried in the sun the next day and the mud was brushed off.

We lacked no conversation for some time thereafter, for everyone had to hear what and how it happened and who was to blame. This of course depended on who was telling the story!

The servants' quarters were fun after any episode in which all angles had to be explained, acted out, all mistakes justified, the misery described in full, and the blame established. Sometimes the servants forgot we had American ears, and the foreign children heard the frank appraisal of the follies and mistakes of the white folk.

Usually the conversation centered around missionaries and their efforts in speaking Chinese, which for us children was as natural as any first language is to a child. The tones of the Chinese were full of pitfalls, as one word could have *very* diverse meanings depending on the tone. The word "*dju*" can mean "God" or "pig" or "bamboo pole" or "to live." It was particularly bad when mistakes were made in preaching! With certain missionaries there were sure to be some hilarious mistakes, which we could enjoy repeating and hearing repeated for some time to come in the servants' quarters.

Chapter 2
Mountain Stream

EVERY SUMMER MOTHER TOOK us to the mountains in Kiangsi Province, a place where missionaries of Central China went to get a cool breath of air and fellowship with other foreign missionaries. For children it was protection against cholera, malaria, dysenteries of many kinds, and other illnesses that threatened in the hot, damp summer months. Missionary mothers usually took to Kuling.

It was a long trip for us. A night and day on the river steamer "plowing" through the mighty and muddy waters of the Yangtze brought us in the late afternoon to a somewhat Europeanized port of Kiukiang, where we took sampans, recklessly bouncing about in the harbor in the wake of launches and ships until we reached the land. The night was spent in the Rest House. It was a house, let us say, where one had to wait overnight for a fresh start to the hills.

Beds were provided in large bare rooms—no mattresses, for we had our own bedding. The rooms were shared with other travelers, and sometimes we had only one bed to a family. Of excitement, noise, lizards on the wall, and general mayhem, there was much; of rest in the Rest House there was none!

In the morning we moved on; our luggage, bedding, and food moved on the backs of coolies and we in sedan chairs—Tsi Si Fu and his wife each in one, Mother in another, and Charles and I tied in together in the fourth, our feet swinging along resting on a board fastened with a chain at each side of the seat.

They tell me that in later years a bus simplified this stage of the journey to Lain Hwa Dong, another rest house, known better as "The Half Way House." I remember it as a lonely place where there was much confusion, much crying and whining for the food and the bedding that had not arrived. It was a place of total exhaustion and little chance to rest. For those who had to stay all night and whose bedding did not keep up, the imprint of the iron springs was branded on all parts of their bodies. They might better have slept on a bed of spikes, but this being China, the naked springs had to suffice! We tried to make the entire trip up the mountain in one day to avoid this punishment.

The path up the mountain was cut out of stone, 3,000 steps up the steep tortuous path, the sedan chairs swinging wildly over precipices. Around and up, around and up we went until suddenly from a cool valley came a blast of invigorating air. This was Kuling—the fairest of hill stations, a refuge from the heat of Central China!

Kuling was the first introduction to other American children for Charles and me. Here we were Americans. Here we went to Sunday school and church where English was spoken. Here we met and learned to love missionaries and their children from many parts of the world.

The Union Church was right across from our mission house with a mountain stream and the main road passing between us, and we could hear the singing at the church while sitting on our wide verandah. We could enjoy not only the concerts put on each year by the community but all the practices as well. As little children the strains of *The Messiah* or *Elijah*, the arias and mighty choruses, were drilled into us just by being in hearing distance.

Our mission owned two houses—one above the other on the mountainside. We had the lower house each year. In those days it went by No. 38A—a prize location in the center of community activities. Mother was hostess of this house. Eighty-one steps above us on the hill was the new mission house, where the Williams family and the unmarried aunties lived as well as other mission personnel. There were woods to play in, mountains to climb, flowers and ferns to collect, birds to watch, and children with whom to play.

Though we lived in the larger house, we as a family occupied only one room. The rest of the house was rented out. There were three other bedrooms and a long living-dining room. The kitchen was out back a little apart, and the cook and his wife had a room next to it.

It was in this multipurpose bedroom of ours, where were a double bed and bunkbeds in one corner nearly filling it, that a little straw cory (suitcase that unfolded and made into a bassinet) was set up. One day while Charles and I were at play, we were invited to enter the semidarkened room and see our baby brother Ezra. It was such a happy event for all of us! But for Mother and Father it was a very great comfort, for here in Kuling, seven years before, their firstborn, a daughter Mary, had been laid away in the foreign cemetery not far away from our summer home.

The people who came to 38A in Kuling to visit or as houseguests had a profound influence on me. Being close to the church, we entertained the visiting lecturers and preachers from many parts of the world, as well as pioneer missionaries. Although we children were young, we shared the richness of their presence.

During the month that Father allowed himself the luxury of being in Kuling with us, he had a Thursday morning Bible study at our house in our one large room. It was filled week by week with missionaries from the hill station who felt the need of this kind of fellowship. Father was the eternal teacher. When it came to medicine, he taught any and all around him who were eager to learn. Everything he discovered of value in his relation to God he shared. He called the group who came weekly to his meetings "The Chain of Witnesses," and he kept in touch with them all year through a newsletter including a sermonette.

Our mission was a small one, and never were there more than two families on the field at one time in my day. The children were all boys except for me—Walter, Jr., Charles, and Ezra. There was little opportunity to play with girls; in fact, there were no girls. My whole world was either Chinese or grown-ups—one composed mostly of aunties of varying ages, temperaments, and degrees of fondness for children. Kuling opened up a whole new world, a world with American children.

Kuling was rich in spiritual teaching for children. The British Children's Special Service Mission was active in Kuling, and meetings were held not in a church or school but out in the stream itself that ran through the hill station. Children were seated on huge rocks that dotted the stream bed. The speaker and song leader were on a higher rock above us. They had a little folding organ with them. I remember they wore Chinese clothes with even the Manchu queue fastened on their caps to look like the Chinese who followed the Manchu custom before 1911.

Father played with us in the stream in front of our house. We floated hand-whittled boats between the rocks. We built dams. We went swimming down at Emerald Pool, where the family came down in the evening for a picnic. We collected everything from beetles to stamps and from butterflies to ferns. Father showed us how to preserve them and had glass-covered boxes made for our better specimens. Even today my brother Charles (with a Ph.D. in botany) is still collecting, trading, classifying, and naming ferns while teaching botany in Taiwan University. The interest and the urge began back in Kuling years ago, and I pause to ponder what good use was made of childhood interests. Soon Father was gone again back to the hospital, while Mother stayed on a bit longer to keep us children out of the heat of the plains.

Chapter 3
Pet Snake and Sudden Storm

THE CHINA INLAND MISSION had a boarding school in Kuling that was just down the road a short distance from our house. When I was six, Mother arranged for Charles and me to stay there after she and our little brother returned to Luho. This was the beginning of the long history of separation of children from parents for the sake of an education now in the third generation. It is traumatic for the child, and, I discovered in later years, for parents also, but there was no other way.

Charles was with me, but I could talk with him only on Saturday. He was number 23, and all my things were marked with the number 41. We wore uniforms of blue serge, and we walked two by two to all our outings as well as to church.

The rules were very strict. There were times for talking and times for complete silence, like in the morning before the gong sounded or in certain halls. It was the silence that awed and frightened me. I had not heard much about silence before, and it was terrifying to me not to be able to talk *at all*! I learned not to break the talking rules the hard way as the punishment was more silence when the rest were at play, and it seemed too heavy to bear to sit with hands over my eyes for a whole hour.

We lined up twice a week to show our knees in case our long black stockings had developed holes. Also, we opened up our mouths to have our throats examined and to answer questions about our health, and while our mouths were open we got one of two kinds of medicine, with the hope that we would stay well.

The principal, Mr. Lindsay, had a large odd box in the main hall in which he kept—of all things—an enormous snake, which we were allowed to view on occasion. One day it got out and we girls were terrified. Eventually it did turn up, and eventually the box was removed, but it seemed an odd pet to be kept at a boarding school. Perhaps it is now stuffed, gracing a glass-enclosed exhibit in some natural history museum! I hope so!

As for the school, however, I only wish there were many more China Inland Mission schools in the world. The loving care, the discipline, and the Christian atmosphere, not to mention teaching, have made a permanent impression of joyous reality, strict rules and pet snakes notwithstanding.

We were not there many months before word came that our parents were going on furlough and we had to leave school before the term was over. There was no one to go with us; Mr. Lindsay called the chair coolies, whom he trusted, and tied us in together, my brother and me, and off we went down the mountain.

We had not gone far when one of Kuling's sudden storms blew up and the rain came down in torrents. In minutes the lovely tranquil and rippling stream at the foot of our Kuling home became a wild, angry torrent sweeping all before it—bridges, rocks, picnickers—as it rushed madly down to the Yangtze River below. But we were not in Kuling, we were on the side of the mountain. Alone! The coolies had run for shelter in a nearby teahouse, setting us down unsheltered in the drenching rain. We were tied in and could not get out, so there we sat while the coolies drank their hot tea and gambled across the tea table.

My brother and I worked at the knots and eventually freed ourselves from the ropes. We then marched into the tea shop and demanded to be taken back to school since we could not go on as we were. The coolies agreed to go back, so before noon we returned, half-drowned and dripping like two forlorn waifs. Since our clothes had all gone on (no telling where that coolie was drinking tea by this time), Mrs. Lindsay took us in and borrowed clothes from the other children to outfit us until our clothes were dry.

The next day we started off once more with the same men, who by now had listened at some length to a lecture by Mr. Lindsay that had the desired effect, for we encountered no tea parties on the trip downhill. At each stop we were met by missionaries who put us in the care of still other missionaries who were taking the steamer to Nanking.

Shortly after my brother and I returned to Luho from our first round at boarding school, it was time for our furlough. This presented problems that seemed insurmountable to my doctor-mother. Sewing was something other women learned to do while she was studying medicine. Furthermore, she had no natural talent for it. She looked over the recent missionary barrel "goodies" that had been put aside, but nothing seemed to be very suitable without extensive remaking for the two boys and me; so she sent for Auntie Holme and the new Auntie Williams. Since both of them knew how to sew, they visited our house one afternoon while Mother outlined for them our needs and showed them her pile of secondhand clothing. Some tolerably suitable clothing evolved with the help of the Chinese tailor, who cut and sewed under the direction of the aunties. There was no foreign child with whom to compare the clothing, and so we were perfectly delighted with whatever emerged from the tailor's hand.

Then there was the matter of the hat. No one had thought of putting a hat in the barrel—there was none. Now it seemed that Auntie Holme had at one time been a seamstress who, with her mother, had done sewing for a living and had some experience decorating hats as well—but a child's hat? She remembered a blue straw that she had worn years before, and another afternoon was taken from the busy mission schedule to convert a woman's hat of many years to a suitable hat for a seven-year-old girl to wear to America. Father insisted that I had to have a hat.

What with Auntie Holme's old blue straw and Auntie Williams' ribbons and bows and flowers and fruit, the most beautiful creation I had ever seen was presented to me for my journey into the fairyland of America.

There were farewells of all kinds: the giving of banners, exquisite silk designs embroidered on silk cloth, black velvet names in Chinese, names of the donor, the recipient and the occasion—all pasted along the sides of the delicate pictures of birds and flowers. There were scrolls and feasts, and finally the day arrived for our departure.

Liu Da Ma, our amah, who had carried baby Ezra strapped to her back and who tried to keep an eye on Charles and me, slipped me a most beautiful brass vase with a dragon encircling it, which is still one of my treasures. She said, "Don't ever forget me," and I never did. We walked with all the missionary family as well as our Chinese family and host of grateful patients, church members, hospital staff, and curious friends to the riverbank, where a little steamer launch was now plying between the Yangtze port of Sha Gwan and Luho.

There were difficulties in going by launch as it was very temperamental. If the river was too high, its wake would break down dikes and flood rice fields. When the river was low the launch would be grounded on a sandbar and there we would sit.

At this time it was the season for floods, but it was finally settled that the launch would go but not come near shore because of the dikes. Off we went amid a great shower of firecrackers and singing of hymns, especially "God Be with You Till We Meet Again." There was also much weeping all around, and finally the steam launch began to move. We waved until all the faces were blurred and finally faded from view.

A brisk breeze blew up as we chugged along, sitting piled up on top of the launch where the passengers were crowded together. We had so hoped that we could make a stop at Gwa Pu, an outstation where Father and Mother had often gone to do dispensary work and there was now a church with some very dear Chinese friends in charge, but the parting visit was not permitted. We only could see them standing on the shore and hear the firecrackers and now and then "God Be with You Till We Meet Again" wafted by the breeze, which was stiffening by the moment.

Wedding picture of George DeVol, M.D. and M. Isabelle French, M.D.—January 17, 1900, at the Friends Mission in Nanking, China.

Isabelle DeVol M.D.

George DeVol M.D.

Luko Hospital, "Peace Hospital"
Father and Mother at the gate
Drs. George and Isabelle De Vol

Morning prayers at Luho Hospital
The De Vol family—in the front row
Attendants and "early bird" patients
sitting behind.

Father with patient
and his staff doing rounds - Luko

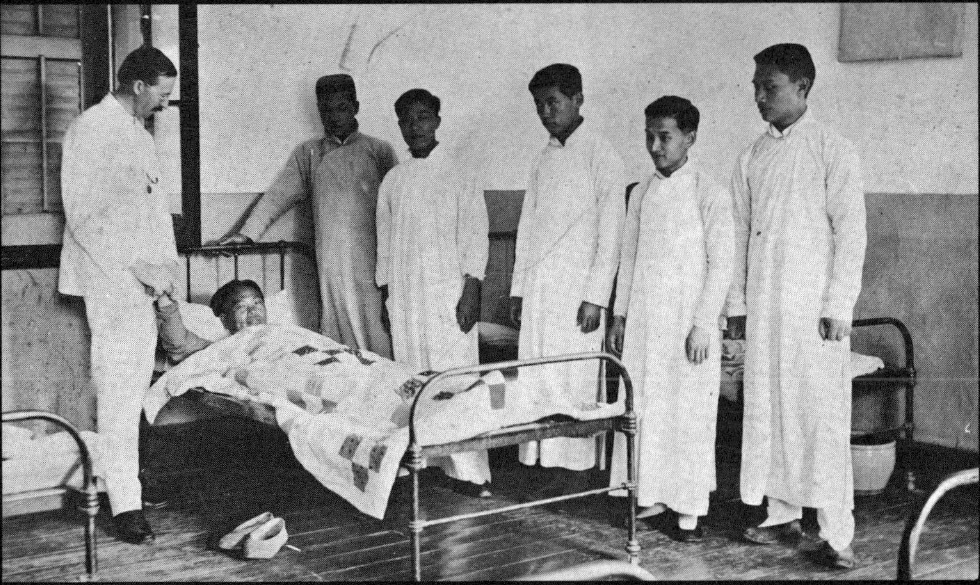

Father with evangelists - Luko

Mother with Catherine and Charles in Luho

Luko missionaries and children. Right: Dr. DeVol and family. Left: Mr. Williams and family. Standing: Margaret Holme

Missionary children in Luko

Catherine and Charles outside the Luko home

Ezra, Catherine, and Charles in their "Christmas chairs" Luko

Three Presbyterian girls and a Quaker (Catherine in center) at home of Dr. Frank Price, Nanking

Quakerage, home for Friends Missionaries in Nanking

Pioneer missionaries in Nanking. Left front: Elizabeth Jenkins, Pres. of Ohio Missionary Society (visitor), Esther Butler, supt. Back row: Margaret Holme, Emma Oliver, Mrs. Shimer (short term), Dr. Lucy Gaynor, Isabella French (mother) and Lena Stanley-girls school.

Charles with Lao Shih the gatekeeper, and goats and cat.

Father and mother's new home at West Gate - Luho

Mother and Ezra after father died in Luho

Father's funeral. Hospital workers. Rev. Gray of Methodist Mission. Walter Jr. Williams, Charles and Ezra barely visible behind Rev. Gray. The casket and Mother's sedan chair.

Chairs following Mother's chair, in which women missionaries were carried in the procession of two miles.

Conscious of my hat, which I held with both hands, I had no hand to wave, but Father felt I should show some enthusiasm for mission workers as well as for my new hat. He gave me a handkerchief and insisted that I wave. At that very moment a breeze came along and lifted my precious beautiful hat off my head and set it down ever so cleverly right in the middle of the Dju River, where it floated some little time and disappeared. I was frantic with disappointment and I wept, for the losing of my lovely hat was at that moment a real tragedy!

It was a great loss to Father as well as to me, for now he insisted that I wear his helmet, a white pith hat far too big for me but necessary, he thought, for protection from the sun. After that, the sooner we got to America the better, as I hated his hat with intensity and humiliation. One of my first and most vivid memories of America was buying a hat in San Francisco. It was also dark blue—a sailor-type with a simple ribbon around it that hung down the back in two smart lengths. It wasn't the flowered beauty the aunties had made, but it seemed that flowers were not seen on little girls' hats that season!

Chapter 4
Roots in the Attic

AMERICA WAS MORE than my childish mind could begin to imagine. We arrived in San Francisco, where Father's brother came to meet us. He was just two years older than Father and looked very much like him; both had black hair and red mustaches. Father had been so long the only man in the mission that to see him walking beside a real brother who was our real uncle was to me more fascinating than the street scenes we passed. Uncle Charles took us to a restaurant down the street away from the docks, as it was noon and there was much to be done about customs and red tape before we could take the train for Santa Rosa, where Uncle Charles lived with his wife and three children and where he pastored a church just next door.

We sat around on our trunks and suitcases all afternoon while customs officials went through our poor belongings. Father was tired and somewhat annoyed at the long delay, and when he was left to put the lids on everything again in order, he said with a sigh, "Blessed be nothing!" How many times have our second and third generations said the same thing when packing time came and especially customs inspection time!

In New York State, Father had another brother and two sisters. One was Aunt Louisa, who with her husband Uncle Harry operated a bakery and lived upstairs over the shop. They had no children but took in three nieces (two of whom were sisters) whose mothers had died years before. Aunt Louisa not only mothered them but employed them in the bakery. We lived with them for some time, accepting their kindness and unselfish sacrifice of space and privacy and in putting up with all the inconvenience and expense of five relatives.

Looking back, it troubles me to think how many times and how many people we have disturbed in our comings and goings through these generations of moving about from East to West and back again! How graciously we have been received and how generously provided for!

Seeing our parents' own people, scenes of their childhood, schools where they went, and teachers whom they cherished began to give an unsettled feeling to us, who thought our roots were in China. The immediate family we were prepared for, but there were cousins and second cousins and second cousins once removed, and then there were friends in all degrees of closeness. We children were bewildered—or let me say, I was! One day Father said to me, "Catherine, I want thee to meet my dear friend ________ ________." I put out my hand to shake his and said in the sweetest manner I could manage, "I am very glad to meet you. I have never heard of *you* before!"

That did it! Father was hurt and ashamed of me, and whatever else he felt, I felt too—later in a different place—but I found other ways of meeting people! It was true I did not know the man, and I was tired of so many people who were so glad to meet the little curiosity from China. Only a very few names had faces when we came to America, but as we came to know people ourselves, the whole matter of people took on significance.

There were no grandparents living when we came to America. This, to me, was a great loss. I had heard so much about Mother's mother in Damascus, Ohio. I saw the farm. We lived there with Mother's brother and family. "This was Grandmother's." "Grandmother always said that . . . ." But not to know her or see her for myself gave me a great sense of loss. I stood in front of the old red brick house where she had lived and tried to imagine what she would be like and what she would say to me, and if perhaps she would give me a sense of belonging in America.

I learned to know her through the old attic door at the farm where Mother's brother lived. Now an attic has very little meaning for those who have never seen one, but suddenly this one became a storybook experience when treasured bits of the past were brought out of the crowded little dark rooms to the light where bit by bit Mother introduced me to her mother.

Grandmother French was a Quaker lady who lived in Ohio. This I knew. That Mother was utterly devoted to her I also knew. I saw the old brick house, which is beautifully kept up even to this day by those to whom it now belongs, and I recognized it and the barn as the scene of many a good-night story in China.

Here in the attic were her Quaker bonnets, no longer in use, but they spoke vividly to me of the past when I saw pictures of her wearing them. There was a silk shawl—white once, but yellowed with age to a lovely creamy softness fringed about with tassels that were thought a little gay and an unnecessary adornment, but I was glad Grandmother had the fringe! There was a quilt made entirely of grey and brown silks and taffetas that once had been Quaker dresses. They were of the finest material in all shades of the two permissible colors pieced together with tiny stitches and so evenly done that it seemed scarcely possible it had all been done by hand. Even the Chinese would have been proud of Grandma's tiny stitches.

Then there were the things that Mother had sent her from China. There was the dainty little Japanese tea set, pink with tiny little blue flowers. Grandma had put it away for me when I came home. The demitasse cups were so delicate—in themselves a treasure—but that they had been Grandmother's, picked out and sent by my own mother, made them more precious to me, and I began to feel a close tie to my mother's mother.

There were also curios from China that were too common to me to notice. Little did I know then that years later after I was grown, after college, after America, after India, after my family was grown, after years of many other places and things, after China's doors were closed, after all missionaries had been gone for years, these little curious reminders of life in China, of the Chinese, my first friends, my first language, my first home would come back to me to be mine and awaken in me the memories that at the age of eight were just forming. I was growing roots in the attic that day.

The summer ended and we started to school, and I was put in the second grade. This was my first year in the second grade, of which there were three years, due to our moving about from one part of America to another. Furloughs play havoc with scheduled education. Furloughs may be an education in themselves but not the kind that shows up on report cards! (We are now experiencing the truth of this for the third generation.)

America was beautiful and people were kind, but my contacts on furlough, as in China, were largely with adults—friends of our parents. I never really knew the children of my own age. There was always the feeling of not belonging. We were constantly on display, and everything we said and did was somehow taken as important when we really just wanted to play and be lost among the other children. This we did not achieve then or ever. We reacted variously to this attention and apartness and felt really more comfortable with the Chinese and other missionary children.

The year was up all too soon, and on the way back to China we were confined to our staterooms. It was 1914. The war was on, and we raced a German destroyer to Hawaii and to safety—but just barely. The *Tenyu Maru* got us on to Japan, but there we had to wait until we could find shipping to Shanghai.

We spent two delightful weeks with Quakers in Japan and then embarked on a Russian ship that took us over the rough China Sea, where this time we were confined to our cabins for other reasons than war! Seasickness is a very real malady where at one stage one fears one will die and then fears one won't! When, however, the lights of China began to appear, we shouted for joy and raised our heads to look out into the night at the twinkling lights that were China.

We were home again, and yet not really at home, because Charles and I had to stay in Shanghai until Christmas, for we were enrolled in the Shanghai American School. Mother and

Father returned to Nanking and Luho. In Shanghai I had my third year in the second grade. There had been too many broken terms in California, New York, and Ohio. Charles and I were together, but we seldom saw each other. It was a comfort to know he was near. In this school we went by names instead of numbers, and we lived in small groups rather than large dormitories. There were eight girls in our apartment. I was the youngest and the least used to living with other girls.

"Catherine, let's turn out the lights tonight and tell ghost stories," said Karis.

"I don't know any."

"Never heard any? You mean you don't adore ghost stories?"

"No," I answered in a thin voice.

"Well, tonight we will get some peanuts on the way home from Hong Kew Park and we will tell you some. It is the greatest fun to dress up like ladies and have a party and after awhile, when Miss Rosebrook turns out the lights, we sit in the dark and tell ghost stories."

As it turned out everyone knew a story but me, but I was their prime audience, and by the time I heard the seventh, I was too scared to go to bed. However, I crawled in and put my foot right in the middle of a soft, slimy coil of something that I supposed was a snake. I screamed and Miss Rosebrook came out of her room to see what was the matter. The girls assured her I was having bad dreams and nothing was the matter. When Miss Rosebrook left I lifted the covers to find mud shaped like a snake and still wet! I was being initiated into boarding school life.

Our first vacation was at Christmas, and S.A.S. students packed the trains into the interior of China with some of us sleeping in the luggage racks and climbing over each other in the 200-mile ride to Nanking, where our parents met us.

It was not a happy vacation for Father and me. I adored him and loved to please him, but this I could not manage to do. I had learned some words that, if not bad, were slang, and Father violently disapproved of slang. The more he called my attention to these words, the more they came to mind, and for each slip of the tongue, I paid dearly. We did an accounting at the end of our vacation, and there was only one day in two weeks I managed to make it through without a spanking.

I love the sound of words and phrases, particularly expressive ones. Why is it that bad ones sound so much more expressive than the plain, solid ones? In any case, my father did what he could to discourage my tendency to pick up the wrong ones!

Father blamed the school in Shanghai for the demoralizing influence on my speech, and I have wondered if perhaps it had something to do with not sending us back for another year. At any rate a school was opened by missionary mothers in Nanking, and though it was a day school, this is where we went thereafter.

Chapter 5

Camphor Tree

NANKING WAS TWENTY-FIVE MILES from Luho. There was a mission house there called the Quakerage, where a number of aunties lived. Mother had lived there herself and had been the doctor in the women's hospital that belonged to the mission. She was also married there in the parlor of the Quakerage five days after Father arrived in China. It had been an occasion to which the American Consul and all missionaries had been invited, and Mother had many friends in the city.

We had visited there many times and even lived there with Mother when she had to relieve some other doctor for furlough, but it had never occurred to us that one day we would live there ourselves, Charles and I, without Mother or Father! The atmosphere was dignified and very proper. It was a large mission house of grey brick with a wide arched veranda across two sides upstairs and down.

The aunties who lived there were pioneer missionaries who had come to China when there was nothing of the mission there and had bought the land and planned every detail of house and yard as well as the girls' school, the women's hospital, the nurses' home, church, and just everything. The compound was beautiful—and the flower gardens, magnolia, snowball trees, camphor trees, and a bamboo grove were artistically set out and became one of the beauty spots of Nanking.

Esther H. Butler was the superintendent of the mission, going out to China with only the vision, courage, and the faith to begin where there were no beginnings. The Quakerage was the name given to the home for missionaries, the plan for which was drawn first in her mind and then on paper and finally built into brick. Her vision went far beyond brick and mortar for a home to the need for a women's hospital, an orphanage for unwanted girls, and later a school, a Bible training school for women.

Esther Butler herself was a tiny little person, neat in her appearance with her hair drawn up severely in the usual missionary knot on the top of her head with combs to keep each hair in place. Though a small woman, she carried herself with tremendous dignity. There was a presence about her that commanded respect of men and women, Americans and Chinese, as well as old and young alike. It was no wonder to those who knew her that she became a friend even of the last Empress of China, and some of the priceless pieces of Chinese art in the Quakerage were gifts from the Forbidden City of Peking.

Auntie Butler, for that is what she was to the missionary children, gathered into the mission other pioneer spirits—selfless women of courage and training who would develop the visions as God gave them.

As Auntie Butler sat with dignity at the head of the table, pouring tea into thin China cups, so Lena Stanley sat at the foot, relaxed and fun loving, serving porridge in the morning and puffed rice at night—the rice being puffed out in the street in hot sand. Auntie Stanley was the teacher of the girls' school and "mother to the orphaned babies." She looked motherly—a large, comfortably built woman with a heart to match.

Along both sides of the always long table were other aunties. Lucy Gaynor was the doctor in the first women's hospital. She was more doctor than auntie, but then some doctors have a way of being busy and a no-nonsense type who are always in too much of a rush to come to meals on time, or tuck in the shirtwaist, or keep rules imposed on the household—the eternal exceptions. However, it was Auntie Gaynor who gave her life caring for refugees after the 1911 war. She was tireless in relief of suffering.

Emma Oliver was everyone's helper, editing the mission paper, overseeing the upkeep of the buildings, meeting emergencies, and purchasing supplies. As aunties go, she was the children's ideal. Her vivid imagination created little creatures and built them into stories that should have been published. We loved the episodes of these furry and feathered folk. Laughter was spontaneous, and she sometimes left the table when she would see the funny side of something not intended to be amusing. She also tipped her chair back, which was against the rules, and all this lack of convention was hilarious for us children. We felt instinctively that not everyone appreciated her, as dignity sat a little uneasily upon her free spirit.

There were language students who rented rooms at the Quakerage. They were single missionaries from America who were temporarily in Nanking, and there were almost always guests.

Personalities of pioneer missionaries were so diverse. It was an education to sit at the table three times a day and observe the idiosyncrasies of each as well as the differences and the strains that sometimes developed and the way they were handled.

There were also degrees in "auntie-hood." Some were so very special and some not too fond of children, and of this we were well aware, though we learned to appreciate them more as we grew older, but all were a part of our mission family. None of them were perfect, I later discovered, and not all decisions may have been wise, but that these were devoted selfless, and strong women of faith no one could ever doubt—not even children.

These were the women with whom we were destined to live so that we could attend the only school for American children in our area.

So it was that the decision was made that Charles and I should live at the Quakerage with the aunties and go to school. It would be closer to Luho. Our parents made infrequent visits on mission business, and we could get home occasionally. Hopefully, we would be under the good influence of our own missionaries, who would keep an eye on us.

I remember well that September day when it was time for us to go to the great walled city of Nanking, move into the Quakerage, and begin life with the aunties.

Long before daylight there were shouts of coolies at the gate of the compound; Lao Shih stumbled sleepily from his great wooden bed and unbolted the gate. There were four men for the chair (for Mother was going with us) and a donkey boy with a donkey that Charles and I would ride—together or in turns. Tsi Si Fu had packed a little lunch and made a nice breakfast. The family was all astir, the servants bustling about, and all three dogs barking, racing around and around the compound as was Jack's and Jill's habit when anything special happened. When all was in readiness at the gate, we kissed little brother Ezra and Father goodbye and were off—Mother in her chair and we children astride the donkey.

Once out of the city gate, we were in the peaceful Chinese countryside. The hot sun was rising, and we jogged along at a rapid, rhythmical pace in the cool, fresh morning air. Willow trees stood knee-deep in water left over from the floods, which had overflowed the banks of the river, threatening the rice fields.

Because of danger to the dikes, the steam launch had ceased to go altogether; hence it was necessary to do the twenty-five miles overland. We walked when we were tired of riding and rode when were were tired of walking. My brother taught me to swim on donkey back. I did the back stroke and side stroke to perfection on donkey back. Somehow, they failed to hold me up once I tried them in water!

It was getting hot late in the forenoon, and there was a town nearby where coolies, donkey, children, and all would stop for a rest and some food. It would be hot rice and hot tea for us at the local teahouse.

We came upon a stream in our path swollen out of its usual narrow bed. To go around would take much too long, so the Chinese decided to try to ford, wade, and scramble. This the chair men managed to do. Charles got across on his own, but I remained on the donkey, and as was my usual fate, the beast slipped and fell in the watery mud and began to disappear. I was rescued from its back, whereupon men on both sides got hold of the tail or head of the donkey, depending on which was nearest at hand, and pulled and tugged until finally the poor animal was able to get on shore, but it was so badly exhausted and covered with mud that Mother excused the donkey and donkey boy, paying a little extra for all their trouble, and they returned home—a somewhat downcast pair.

Refreshed by the hot food at the teahouse, we were again ready to travel, but the chair coolies had discovered a traveler who wished to go back to Luho. This they were glad to do—for more than we had bargained for—so now Mother was suddenly without means of travel as were children. After much shouting and bargaining, four men were found who would carry Mother on, and with the afternoon heat upon us, we children walked the remaining miles to the city, stopping now and then for tea as we passed a village and eating a pomegranate in the shade of a welcome tree. Several hours of hot sun and thirteen cups of tea later, we arrived at Pu Kao, a city across the Yangtze River from Nanking.

The closer we got to Nanking, the more apprehensive we became. Mother had so wanted us to look and behave suitably when we arrived that night, but the hot day and unexpected drag of the miles on our spirits did not make any of the three of us any more comforted. "You must not be any trouble to the aunties. It is very good of them to have you. Remember: try to be quiet. The aunties are not accustomed to children, so be very good; I know you will." Thus Mother counseled us.

The long rickshaw trip was nearly over. I was cuddled up with Mother in hers while Charles raced along behind with piles of luggage. The coolies ran most of the way along the wide city streets of the great city. At last we passed through the city gate and were set down at the Quakerage entrance. We were welcomed with quiet dignity to life with the aunties.

Charles was given the office where new missionaries had struggled with the Chinese teacher. A cot was set in it and it became his room. It opened out through French windows to the lovely yard where the camphor tree stood with open arms inviting us to climb her branches and make her our playhouse and retreat. He had the whole of the compound outside the door of his room—the only bedroom downstairs. The birds were his to study and stuff. The trees and garden were his to watch and to love, and I was his constant companion as he was mine.

My room was for one year in Auntie Stanley's girls' school. I lived in the storeroom. The Chinese girls were in the room across the hall in the large dormitory; Auntie Stanley had her suite nearby. The girls were not allowed to go to their rooms during the day, so neither was I, but I did not realize this. Soon after we went to live with the aunties, my brother and I had gathered up the fall leaves and made a great pile of them. We then buried each other under the leaves so that nothing of us showed. When one was resurrected the other was buried. It held great attraction for us, for we both loved the leaves. There was so much we could do with them.

The leaves, however, were matted into my hair with dust all over me. There were leaves in my ears, in my clothes, and I was really a fright. I wished to take a bath, but there was no provision for that except on certain nights, and furthermore the door to the upstairs rooms was locked, and there was no provision either for changing rules for any private emergencies.

I did what I could in my brother's room, but Un Bao, the cook, said we were having company—very special guests for dinner that night. Charles's other door opened onto the kitchen verandah, and we could see it was true. What agony of humiliation I felt that night as I sat beside the gentleman guest! He turned out to be the pastor of the Foreign Union Church, and his wife, the principal of the school at Hillcrest! How miserable children can be! How ashamed the aunties must have felt also!

I have tried in my mind to fix this situation over and over again, but at that time there seemed to be no solution but to sit there with leaves scratching everywhere and in no way disguised. Obviously the rules had not been made with fall leaves in mind —nor for resurrection excitement! We learned to do less dramatic things, and eventually when autumn turned the leaves of the lovely snowball tree to red and orange and yellow, I pressed them and gave them to Mother for her birthday. We still climbed the camphor tree, but the dried leaves were gathered and burned.

There must have been more problems connected with my living with the Chinese girls than I realized, because the next year I was put in the Quakerage at the end of a long hall in the trunk room. It was at the top landing of the back stairs used by servants who emptied slops and brought up bath water, and the door at the end of the upstairs hall was locked at night, separating me from the rest of the house. I used to love to hear the nurses coming to call the doctor or any sound of human activity that I recognized. Otherwise I was terrified to go to bed. I never knew which was best—to lock the screen and leave the door open so I could hear the aunties going into the bathroom or to lock the door and be safer from real danger but further away from people.

Charles always went upstairs with me. We looked under the bed and behind the curtain that hid my clothes. When all seemed as usual, Charles went downstairs slowly as we repeated each night the ritual we adopted just in case:

"Good night, Charles."

"Good night, Catherine."

"Forgive me if I did anything wrong to you today."

"Yes, forgive me, too."

"Good night."

"Good night."

And then from the bottom of the stairs,

"Good night."

I then read the Scripture, which always happened to open at John the fourteenth chapter, "Let not your heart be troubled." Mother had armed me with two verses that I was to quote at such times as this: "What time I am afraid, I will trust in thee." For me it was every night that I was afraid. The other verse was: "I will trust and not be afraid," but it was not as meaningful to me at first since I already was afraid. Those verses have never been forgotten as Mother intended they should not be. How grateful one can be when a weapon against fear is built into one's reflexes! Peace would come, and a good night was usually the result. And, of course, we had the prayer

Father gave us to pray, and this we did—rapidly, but faithfully. God knew what we were going to say anyhow, so it did not matter how fast it went, and sometimes we said it slowly and thought about it and about home and wept a little into the pillow.

A little pond and a parade ground away from the Quakerage was the Union Seminary Compound, where a row of mission houses stood. These homes were opened to the children of Presbyterian missionaries, who also came to Nanking to attend Hillcrest. In one home especially we found our dearest childhood friends. It was the home of Dr. Frank Price and his wife, the same couple who had come to dinner the night we had played "resurrection from the grave of leaves." They had several sons, of whom only two were left in China. The youngest, Harry, became the closest friend of Charles. They also kept three girls who were my age—Nettie, Evy, and Margaret, whom we called Pat.

Pat and I understood each other perfectly, as her mother was also a doctor and we both had secondhand clothes trouble. Walking back and forth to school, she and Harry and Evy and Nettie would join with us as we chased each other over the mounds of graves between our mission homes and the school. Now and then we stepped down into a coffin whose wooden lid had mingled with the dust, leaving only the white dry bones of the skeleton to crunch under our blundering feet. There was no marker to say whom we trod upon or in what century he—or was it she?—had been laid to rest at this spot, which had been invaded first by time and now by the "foreign devils" on the way to school!

Chapter 6
"Distress on Horseback"

NANKING WAS A GREAT CITY, towered over by Purple Mountain, outside the city wall. Drum Tower was the entrance with three arched gateways. The center one was much larger for the carriages and big wagons. The smaller one on each side was for pedestrians, bicycles, and rickshaws, wheelbarrows, and donkeys. The University of Nanking was at the Drum Tower as also was the University Hospital, which attracted professors, doctors, and people of many nationalities with their families.

The foreign community in Nanking was very large, and we had teachers at Hillcrest from among wives and mothers who were talented and admirably trained to teach the children of the community.

We had a Literary Club called Watch Guard, which met once a month in one or the other of the mission compounds, though never at the Quakerage. We wrote poems, essays, stories, sang, and performed in all kinds of ways for the parents who lived in the city. We all took part. I recall once my assignment was to give an essay on Saturn. Auntie Butler took this very seriously and gave me books to read on the subject. I then wrote out an essay upon it, which she carefully edited. I was then to learn it by heart. This I practiced every afternoon in Auntie Butler's apartment.

Auntie Butler had become so interested in my progress that she decided to put all else aside and attend Watch Guard so that she could report to my parents how well I was doing.

I had not expected to see her there, so when I stood up, speech well in hand, I was so nervous and frightened that I shook all over and remembered only the first paragraph and the last. All the labor that had gone into describing the important details of the rings around Saturn was lost. All the hours of practice were wasted, and I came back to the Quakerage in utter humiliation. The air was stiff with disapproval.

Auntie Butler was never more human and lovable than when she was annoyed—so long as her annoyance was caused by someone else beside my brother or me.

The dusting was done at the Quakerage before breakfast, and Auntie Butler inspected the job, particularly on Thursdays, because on that day the missionary ladies of the city came to our Quakerage parlor for prayer meeting.

On one Thursday morning I was up early and watched the woman dust. Along came Auntie Butler and picked up a picture over the mantle. It was a scene of water and sky, but Li Da Ma never knew which was which, and it usually ended up with sky and water reversed. "Li Da Ma, thee come here," she said in half Chinese and half English. She explained about the water and sky and told her how to tell which was which and not to make the mistake again. And then to me on the side, "It looks like distress on horseback!"

I was utterly delighted with this unexpected abandon on the part of dignified Auntie Butler. It seemed to me far too exciting to have it happen only once; thereupon I rose early when in need of a bit of sparkle in the daily monotony and turned the picture upside down if perchance Li Da Ma had learned right side up.

Auntie Butler always noticed. The effort was never lost nor did it fall flat. Li Da Ma was brought in and told again—poor confused soul—and I got the shocking rough language I loved so much, "It looks like distress on horseback."

April Fool was a new idea to us. We learned about it at school on the morning of the first day of April, when for the first time lies and false impressions and tricks seemed to go unpunished and indeed to be expected. This was an opportunity not to let pass—so Charles and I had one of our conferences.

How was this to be shared with our dignified aunties? How far could we go? We had heard of only a few ideas, so there was not too much variety of possibilities. In the end, Charles tied the dining room chairs to the one opposite so no chair could be pulled for sitting down after grace. I put salt in the sugar bowl and sugar in the salt shaker. We got Un Bao the cook to promise not to tell. It was a wild thing for him to do. As it turned out, it was all a little wild and not very successful.

Miss Butler stood by her chair and gave it a pull. It did not give. She tried again, this time with effort. It did not move.

"Charles," she said sternly and with no amusement, "thee please to untie these chairs."

Charles untied the chairs and that was all there was. No one laughed. The sugar and salt were sent out, which was what Un Bao thought would happen, and we were left to wonder what was so funny about April Fool. At the Quakerage—it fell flat!

Life at the Quakerage was adult. The aunties who occupied the four bedrooms upstairs were pioneering, each in her own field. Visitors from all over China and other parts of the East passing through Nanking stopped at the Quakerage. The fact that we children were also there was incidental and an unavoidable necessity, and not too troublesome so long as we all kept the rules.

Auntie Butler was a highly respected member of the Nanking community. She was principal of the first women's Bible training school, which was a union project. She was an excellent Bible teacher herself, and her executive ability and knowledge had secured for her a place on many interdenominational committees and boards. Her desk was piled high with important papers of all categories, for she was also the superintendent of the entire Friends Mission as well. Her filing system was at times inadequate; she spread her papers about the room in piles, and only she knew which pile was important and which was not.

My room was seldom required for mission use—being at the back of the house and locked off from the main part, but now and again I was asked to relinquish it for guests and share

Auntie Butler's bed with her. Her room was cozy with a fireplace and bath of its own. It was really a great honor to share it with her, and I loved to be asked, though I was expected to be as unobtrusive as a child could be and my things had to be put away neatly in a small space.

One day during a conference when I was removed from my usual abode to her room, I found her after school in great distress looking frantically for papers—very important ones—that were nowhere to be found.

"Catherine, has thee seen the papers?"

"No," I replied, "I haven't seen any special papers—just the ones lying about on your desk."

"Thee hasn't touched any papers?"

"No."

"Did thee carry out the wastepaper basket?"

"No, but the amah did. I saw her."

"That's where they were," she cried out in exasperation. "Doesn't thee know that I keep my important papers in that basket!"

I have pondered this since—but however it was, Auntie Butler was human as well as austere and was capable of laughing at her own absurdities. There was something about her tiny dignified person that commanded respect, and she had it from me. She did not once give in to weakness, and she did not expect me to give in to my weakness either. There was a right way to do everything, and she expected me to find it. Her own self-discipline seemed to draw out the very best in those about her.

One night my usual fear and uneasiness in going to bed alone mounted to terror. I had been introduced to Scrooge by one of the new missionaries who came to live at the Quakerage. I had never heard of the gentleman before, and I could hear the chains rattling on the back stairs. My heart was beating wildly, and I knew that if I got help from anyone it would have to be before the door was locked, so I rushed down the hall and knocked timidly at Auntie Butler's door. She let me in and sat me down by the cozy, comforting fire, for it was December. "What is on thy mind?" she queried. I told her about

Scrooge and the chains and how I could hear them on the stairs and I could not sleep.

"Thee count thy blessings," she said simply.

Well, there was Mother and Father and a good home and the good aunties who had so kindly let us come to live with them. There were the usual comforts of life, and after a little while I had quite a list of things for which a little girl, scared out of her wits, might be thankful. I made it as long as I could while all the time I was hoping, perhaps even praying, that she would break down and say, "All right, Catherine, thee can sleep with me tonight."

But this she did not say. What she said was, "Now thee go back to bed, Catherine." So we had a word of prayer and that was all.

Looking back at that moment of disappointment I see the wisdom of her words. Had I crawled into bed with her, as I so wanted to do, I might have expected it again and again when I was afraid. I have called her method "strong consolation" rather than the comfort I wanted.

Dr. Li Yuin Tsao was a Chinese doctor, American trained. She was beautiful, dedicated, and efficient. She was the doctor now at the women's hospital and the only Chinese auntie in the house. She tried to raise the standard of health and general well-being of her sister Chinese, who now and then disappointed her and refused her help, the customs of centuries being stronger. Occasionally she would come to the table with some such let-down. Perhaps a patient had left the hospital before the scheduled operation . . . or maybe another had removed a bandage, infecting the wound . . . or one had taken the wrong medicine or in wrong amounts . . . . Her expression invariably was: "These Chinese!"

This offended me, as I felt personally insulted. What was wrong with us Chinese? I never doubted that I was one of them, and it seemed to me that Dr. Tsao was letting us all down. I have discovered since that educated nationals are inclined to be less tolerant or patient with the ignorance among their own people than "foreign" missionaries are.

During the visit from a missionary from India on her way home for furlough, there was a very pressing meeting in Luho. It was imperative for all the missionaries on the field to be there. All the aunties went, leaving the visiting missionary, Carrie Wood, in charge at the Quakerage.

She was a very quiet, gentle person, very lovable, and I took to her right away, fascinated with tales about India, which seemed unbelievably backward and yet romantic.

One morning I was late to breakfast. "Catherine, there is one thing upon which I insist. You must be on time for breakfast. I am very uneasy when you are late. How do I know if you died in the night!" That was a thought—one I had never thought of. I had been afraid of many things, but that was a new one. I woke up early thereafter, largely out of curiosity, I think. I wanted to be sure I was alive!

We had many happy visits together. I was not late again. Little did I know that she would one day be Auntie Wood—not only to me but to my children as well in the far-off, fantastic India.

Thursday afternoon at four the women missionaries of Nanking came to the Quakerage for prayer meeting. Tea often preceded it, and it was a very pleasant and inspiring interlude. We children were invited to attend. There was a period when no one present would play the piano and I was accorded the position of pianist. We sang "Trust and Obey" until I learned one or two more hymns for variety. Auntie Butler was very pleased at this accomplishment, and I was pleased that she preferred piano—even only my one song—to the nimble guitar with many tunes strummed by the language student rooming with us at the Quakerage.

It seems to me now that perhaps hearing grown-ups in prayer in honest confession and heart-searching was the most valuable part of our life at the Quakerage aside from the sheer business of discipline. Prayers and answers were sometimes not far apart, and the example of dedication to one's call and vision was indelibly imprinted upon two homesick children living with the courageous women who were bravely attempting to push back darkness in an alien land.

The visits Father or Mother made to Nanking were few and always on business, but they were treasured moments. There was so much to tell and so much to ask about.

One night after a big feast when crabs were served, I was desperately ill, alone in my outside room. New missionaries had just arrived and passed my door to and from the bathroom. The sounds coming from my room gave them an eerie start in missionary life, and I'm sure they wondered what ailed the little girl, but no one stopped in. Toward evening I looked up from my misery to see my mother's face—I could scarcely believe my eyes. There stood Mother, doctor, nurse, all in one; and she took over. What miracle had brought her to me at the hour when I needed her so much? What Loving Heart had sent her? I was content just to know she was there!

Chapter 7

A Grey Blanket over the Valley

IT WAS DECEMBER AGAIN and time to return to Luho. We went part way by boat and were met by coolies with Mother's sedan chair with a brass footwarmer in it and some food for us to eat. We were to travel the rest of the way in the chair together. There was also a note that the bearers gave us.

It said, "Father is very ill. Be very quiet when you get home. We are longing to see you. Love, Mother."

The thought of Father's illness was a very sobering one. He was never ill. Homecoming was never quiet. We all shouted to each other and to the servants, and the dogs barked and raced around the house in wild abandon. How does one go home quietly? We tried to subdue our voices in genuine concern, but the dogs were as wild as ever, yet we went to the house very apprehensively because Father's illness was obviously a reality. I read concern in Mother's face, and the servants and other missionaries who came to help seemed anxious.

We tiptoed upstairs to see Father, and it was very apparent that he was indeed ill. It seemed that at church where he preached the Sunday before, he had noticed a very aggravating sore on the back of his neck. This developed into a carbuncle that spread to the glands on his neck. He lost his voice and could speak only in whispers. There was something awesome about the atmosphere of our home. There was nothing of the Christmas we had expected. Doctors were sent for from Nanking. All the hospital and Christian community and finally the surrounding missionary community were involved in the growing crisis.

Charles stayed beside Mother. He was fourteen when we came back on that trip from the Quakerage, but in the few days that followed, he became a man, standing beside Mother and keeping vigil with Father.

I went to stay with Auntie Holme, and our younger brother Ezra with the Williams family.

Auntie Williams felt it was really too bad to have Christmas come and go with no celebration at all; so she invited us all to her home on the 26th. As it happened, there were no gifts from America that year. Since no boxes had arrived, she sent out to the street and had some gift for each one present. It was a very memorable evening, though a heaviness hung over us all. Mother remained with Father, and the doctors and helpers continued their efforts to stop the ravages of the growing infection.

Auntie Holme and Auntie Williams carried through the Christmas carols, the dinner, the gift-giving. My gift was a teapot, grown-up size but all mine, and for some reason it was a perfect choice. I enjoyed being given a household item like these dear aunties used rather than a small imitation, as toys are meant to be. The brown teapot was the one bright spot in the saddest Christmas one could imagine.

Auntie Holme took me to see Father each day. One day we found the evangelists in his room, so I waited downstairs by the fireplace. When the men came down, they were very broken with emotion. They had helped him up in a sitting position and with his hoarse and breaking voice, he gave them his last message.

At another time the entire hospital staff gathered around Father as he told them that he was sure that God was calling him and that they must carry on his work. He told them how it should be done and gave to them his last message. Charles did not leave Father. I heard none of these last words, but Charles stood there with the hospital workers and heard his father commit this vision and concern to Chinese men.

These were the men Father had loved and trained. They were his constant daytime companions, and three of them in particular looked upon the foreign doctor as their own father. They loved him and they spent the last hours with him. Father was conscious, and as the disease took a firmer grip on his life, there was less pain; so Father and Charles had a talk together in the early hours of the last Sunday morning.

Missionary friends from Nanking gathered in to be near Father. A missionary doctor who had been the best man at his wedding now came to fight for Father's life. The missionary community was a very close fellowship that crossed all denominational lines.

Auntie Holme kept me with her. She talked to me long hours at night as I began to feel that an ominous crisis lay ahead. I slept with her at night, and on the Sunday morning of December 30, 1917, while the church service was going on, I sat with Auntie Holme by the fire while she told me of the great host of fatherless children whose fathers had died in the war and how brave they had to be to help their mothers through their loss as well as their own. She was telling me this when Auntie Williams came down and said, "Catherine, your father is safe in heaven." Then came Mother and Charles with her, stumbling down the stairs. I heard her say, "This beautiful chapter of my life is closed." Little Ezra was upstairs, and he heard his mother weeping.

Mother and Father had been such lovers. He spoke to her and of her with the greatest respect. He called her "Dr. Isabella," and she spoke of him as "Dr. George," except when they were alone. They had depended entirely on correspondence for their developing romance because they had just found each other a few weeks before Mother left for China when she was speaking in New York to Young Friends at Yearly Meeting. Father chanced to attend that night. He had a medical practice in Staten Island and was also planning to go to China as a medical missionary. He was eager to meet this Miss French, M.D., who was about to set out for what was exactly his life goal. In their brief conversation it became apparent that they had both been to the same college but to different medical schools. Both had graduated and interned and both were headed for the same mission in China.

Romance was sparked but had to be carried forward to engagement and plans for marriage all by letters, since Mother left soon after for China and Father had two years of practice before he could pay off his debts and get free to go. Thus their marriage took place five days after his arrival in Nanking in 1900.

I knew much about the details of their love because I had found the love letters in Mother's old round-top trunk in the little storeroom of our little house in Luho. Mother and Father had to be away most of the day—all morning except when at 10 o'clock Mother ran back across the street to see if we children were playing nicely. She usually stirred a few acetic acid crystals into boiled water that had been cooled in a basket let down into the well. This made a quick lemonade and gave her a little respite between rounds at the clinic. While she was away, there were rainy days and dull days and sick days when there seemed to be nothing to do. The amah was busy with little Ezra, and Charles was collecting his stamps, birds, butterflies, bugs, or stones.

I read Mother's letters. I was discovered and told not to ever read those letters again until I had a romance of my own, but already I had read enough to think of them as the most beautiful letters in the world. They were restrained and yet full of love and longing, stories of incidents on both sides of the ocean—Chinese experiences and American ones. They told each other of interesting medical cases. They made plans and they missed each other, agonizingly, but each carried on until the 17th of January, when they were married in the Quakerage with these same friends to share in their greatest day of joy who now shared in her hour of sorrow.

One evening near the end, Mother came into the room and stood at the foot of the bed. Father looked up at her and asked:

"Mother, did we ever lack for anything?"

She stood for a moment and replied, "Never." That was the end of the conversation, but those of us who heard it have never forgotten it and have done a lot of thinking about it ever since.

From the moment it became certain that Father would not recover, plans for his coffin were begun. It was lined with a lovely soft white Chinese silk and covered on the outside with black. The coffin was kept in Mother's downstairs study, where Chinese streamed in all hours of the day to see that man who had loved them, healed their bodies, and brought the message of life to their souls.

The funeral was on the second of January on the verandah of the hospital. White coarse cloth was hung up twisted into patterns like a screen in Chinese fashion to close off a large open space where hosts of Chinese crowded in to pay their last respects. Mr. Gray took charge of the crowds of people, welcoming them. We, the mourners, were draped with white bands with a black strip down the center. This we wore across one shoulder and fastened under the opposite arm.

Our Chinese pastor, Pastor Gao from Nanking, took charge. He also had come to Luho days before Father's death and had preached the sermon on the Sunday morning in the local church, where Father had so often preached. His sermon was "Lord, he whom thou lovest is sick." Today he preached to the huge crowd of Chinese.

The funeral procession formed after the service. The men mourners went behind the banner bearers, who were members of the church: Charles, little Ezra, Walter Williams and his son, the foreign visitors, and the three hospital helpers—Wang Chuen'-Hua, Lui Yuen-Chiao, Lee Sheo-Dao—who had given Father the respect and honor they would give to their own fathers. The relation of father and son was not lightly passed on to others. It was a sacred relationship. Sons of the family had responsibility to carry on the family tradition, religion, good name; and this loving duty was not assumed by just anyone. These three Chinese men mourned with us as part of our family, and it was to us right that it should be so.

Behind the men came the casket carried by eight men all in white mourning gowns and white caps. Mother followed behind in a closed sedan chair. I sat behind her with Auntie Holme, the missionary women, Auntie Williams, Dr. Tsao, and many others of our friends.

Behind them filed the hundreds of Christians who made up the hospital staff, church officials, school teachers, the students from the boys and girls school, the patients who had been helped at the hospital, the city dignitaries, officials, the beggars, and thousands of people who filled up the entire city streets, pushing onlookers into stores and all open spaces. It was a mile outside the West Gate to the little cemetery—out in the country among some fields, and the only other white person laid there was little Grace Williams, who had died at the age of two. She was the only other American girl to be born in Luho, and she had died while we were on furlough.

Never before had the city of Luho seen such an impressive procession. The young doctor who had come to them as a stranger with his wife had won the hearts, the respect, and love of the people throughout the entire district, and his death was a great blow to rich and poor.

Everything was done the Chinese way and in the Chinese language, and it was the only way that would have seemed right to us, for we were far more at home in Chinese Luho than in the semi-foreign life of Nanking.

However, the foreigners who were there were a great comfort to us all. They gathered at our house after the funeral to talk over future plans. They insisted that Mother and Ezra return to Nanking with us. Dr. Tsao was there and Pastor Gao. They were as much a part of our council as any other. Dr. Tsao lived with us for a week and returned with us to Nanking while the pastor took the place of shepherd to the stricken community during the whole period. His presence was a great comfort to Father to the end and a strength to us during this period of sorrow.

Nothing was ever the same again. Charles, who had scarcely left Mother's side or Father's either during the last days, was no longer a boy. He had given his father some shells for his gun for Christmas. The "boy" in him was hoping Father would be able to use them soon, for he loved hunting. He apologized that he did not have money to buy more.

"This is fine, Charles," he said, "quite enough for this Christmas." And so they were. But Charles was now thinking of Mother and how to help her with us children. Before we knew it we were thinking of him as Mother's helper, and we listened to him with seriousness and a little awe, for Charles was not just Charlie—one of us—anymore!

There was so much beauty, so much love, so much security in the concern of foreigners of all denominations, such sorrow in the hearts of Chinese, that the experience of that Christmas vacation was not terrifying to me. Death would not be a thing to fear. For Father it was really a glorious promotion. All that he had preached was a reality to him in the hour of death and to Mother in giving her poise and peace and quiet acceptance. Christian fellowship was a real experience to us all; and victory, love, and hope were the dominant notes that even a child could understand.

For six months afterward, I wept each day. I loved Father. He was severe and strict and expected the best from us, but he loved us and we loved him. I remember the day months later when I suddenly realized that I had not cried all day long. But we learned to live again and found life at the Quakerage pleasant with Mother and Ezra there with us.

In March, Mother and Ezra returned to Luho, where Mother opened the hospital again with necessary limitations. It was a very lonely life for the two of them. Ezra found comfort in his teddy bear, which was to him what Winnie-the-Pooh was to Christopher Robin. It was his constant friend by day, a bedfellow by night. Mother taught him when she had free moments from the hospital; and Walter Junior (Williams) and he had hours of play together, which usually included time out for violent differences between them.

Shortly after Mother returned to Luho, the pneumonic plague broke out in Nanking, and all schools were closed, including Hillcrest.

It was a terrifying experience to look out from the upstairs verandah at the road we used to go to school each day, used now to carry dead bodies out to be disposed of. Masks were ordered for all who went outside their homes, and the Quakerage was turned into a mask factory, for everyone who was free helped to make masks. Rickshaw men wore them, and policemen and all who had to be on duty. Finally a decree went out that the city gates were to be closed and all who wanted to leave the city must do so on one certain day, beyond which there could be no possible way to leave.

The aunties talked it over at the Quakerage and decided to send us to Luho, since the school was closed and there was no way to tell how long we would be there idle. Perhaps it was safer in Luho. At least we could be with Mother, so we started out with a servant—the three of us masked—to Sha Kuan, where we got a houseboat on to Hwa Dz Keo.

We arrived in Luho to find that the plague had reached Luho as well, and Mother and the hospital workers were busy making masks. The pneumonic plague hit the lungs and killed within hours. It spread from one city to the other, but Luho was spared any real epidemic, for it passed quickly, and before long we were back at school again. It did, however, give us some wonderful days with Mother and our little brother, who was exceedingly lonely, as even his little friend, Walter Williams, had gone to Shanghai to school.

The last of June we went to Kuling, taking with us Pat, my chum. Mother was ill herself, and soon after her arrival in the beautiful Kuling mountains, she was taken to the hospital, where she remained most of the summer.

After Mother became ill, Myrtle Williams took over the lower bungalow as hostess and took care of us three there as part of her family. It was a sad summer, and she did everything to make it a bit happier.

Mother was in the hospital at the China Inland Mission compound just down the road a little way from us, and we went to see her each day. She had sprue, an Oriental disease of the entire alimentary tract, and she was very weak. It had been too much for her to try to carry on the hospital alone, and yet she had kept hoping.

No one can live in inland China and not be aware of the great work of the China Inland Mission. Their headquarters were in Shanghai, and we always stayed there for a few days when we traveled to and from America or had business in the big city. They kept a sort of hotel for missionaries, and each night after dinner all guests gathered for prayers. For some reason I loved these times as a tiny girl. I felt so safe, so happy, and so exalted when these missionaries spoke or prayed and, especially, sang. So now in Kuling, Mother was in their care once more, and I visited them not only to see her but to share in the worship with Mother in the same atmosphere I loved so much.

Mother had a way with people. People came to her for advice—medical often, but it usually led to deeper problems. She had secrets that she never told. Everyone trusted her. Young brides talked to her, and brides-to-be sought her out. Everywhere Mother was, someone came to her for help, even in the hospital when she herself was a patient.

Life on the Kuling Mountain was idyllic that summer. There were so many things to do, places to go, whether to the valleys and streams below or to the hills and mountains above.

A walk on the ridge behind our house came to an abrupt end where a Buddhist monastery hidden among caves and bamboo groves overlooked the plains and the Po Yang Lake, which was a widened part of the Yangtze River. In the middle was an island where storied pagodas rose to pierce the summer sky.

From that distance no life could be seen—just a lovely Chinese picture in miniature, whether one looked to the mountain from whence we had come or down to the sheer drop to the plains; it was awe-inspiring, peaceful, remote, and just such a place to contemplate for a lifetime. The priests, clad in their grey robes, lived in that silence with only the sound of temple bells to interrupt their meditation. It was like standing at the edge of one world and looking down upon another far below.

I was only twelve then, but I had long thoughts. With Father gone and Mother ill, life began to show its serious side, as well as its beauty. Nowhere could one find a more charming setting for awaking to reality. The little foreign settlement was the queen of summer resorts. Chinese mountains look different from other mountains, not so rugged or barren as the higher mountains of West China.

I loved the mountain gorges, the rushing streams, the waterfalls and wooded hills, the mist settling down like a grey blanket over the valleys, the sudden flash storms rushing from nowhere, cool air, delightful fellowship, the sound of thousands of cicadas (locusts) grinding in unison. I remember the great chorus of missionary voices singing the stirring oratorios. . . . Lilies were everywhere, ferns and birds, a paradise of natural beauty, sunsets of Chinese red splashed across the sky trimmed with gold—this was Kuling.

Chapter 8
Farewell, Bamboo

LIFE BEGAN AS USUAL at the Quakerage. Mother was transferred to the Missionary Union Hospital in Nanking, where Auntie Butler joined her. Both were very ill, and Charles and I were taken in by other missionaries.

There were enough foreign students by that time to have all kinds of activities. Hillcrest School now had a full-time teacher from America, and we had learned how to live happily in the Quakerage with the aunties, but Mother did not improve. It was 1918. The armistice was signed November eleventh, and on the eighteenth our little family secured passage from Shanghai to return to America. Mother was too ill to carry on her medical work and was now a patient herself, so the emergency health furlough was imperative.

A missionary lady was mentally ill and had to be accompanied to America by a physician. Auntie Stanley was also ill with sprue, which was what Mother had; so although Mother was very ill herself and returning for health reasons, she had two patients under her care.

It was characteristic of life among missionaries to impose on each other, but no one called it that. Indeed, I never heard the word in connection with favors until we came to America. Missionaries looked after one another and helped one another, particularly in isolated places. If someone went to Shanghai to the dentist, she expected to take a long list of errands to help the others left behind.

Thus it was no imposition for Mother, ill though she was, with three children, to take a demented woman (whose sole desire was to end her misery in the ocean) to America along with Auntie Stanley.

We gathered at the railway station at Nanking, Mother with her brood of three children and two sick women. The Chinese friends, servants, fellow workers, our dear Pastor Gao, the missionary families, the aunties, and a host of Hillcrest friends were there.

Among them stood Uncle Walter, Aunt Myrtle, and our only mission playmate, Walter Williams, Jr. The young lad stood silently watching the drama, instinctively realizing he would never again see our mother and wondering what was going to happen next. The air was heavy with grief as the time came for the puffing engine to move.

Charles took in the situation and, with gesture of command, climbed the steps to the train and called out: "ALL ABOARD!" Many years later Walter, Jr., said, "That was the perfect gesture, which put emotions and situations back into perspective again, relieving the pressure building up on the platform." And the small party waving from the train windows, as Nanking faded from our view, turned to practical matters of finding seats on a crowded train.

The passage to Japan was rough; Mother, Lena Stanley, and I were seasick. This left Charles delegated to watch over the mentally ill member of our party and Ezra also, occasionally looking in on the rest of us. He had no time for the usual shipboard activities suited to a fifteen-year-old.

Eventually I arose from the state of seasickness to help watch one or the other. We had traveling companions of all kinds. The missionaries had services each morning. The walkers walked around the deck; the shuffle-boarders shuffled; the dancers danced; the drinkers drank; the gamblers gambled; and children flooded the boat, hiding in lifeboats and romping everywhere, and the seasick? They did what came naturally! Before long, everyone found his own society. What with guarding the rail to prevent a possible suicide, or waiting on the sick, or entertaining little brother, our family kept busy.

A businessman from Shanghai took in the situation and, at Honolulu, took us ashore and gave us a wonderful day at Waikiki Beach with swimming and ice cream, and a gift to remember the day. Mine was a brooch with the Hawaiian seal on it, which I kept as one of my favorite things for many years.

The Hillcrest School family of teachers and schoolmates had sent gifts and letters along with us to be opened one each day for the entire journey. In that way they went with us, cheering us along until we reached San Francisco.

Our depressed charge got progressively worse; and, after some days out at sea, she was committed to a padded cabin for safekeeping.

Upon our arrival in San Francisco, we children turned our attention to the America that we knew so slightly but which was to be our home until the doors to the East were opened to us again.

My brothers both were destined to return to China, Nanking and Luho, and live through the upheaval of those difficult war years—sometimes driven out, sometimes carrying on their work: Charles in Luho Academy as its principal and Ezra as surgeon in Nanking. Eventually both were evacuated. Little did I know then that I was destined to return to the Orient by way of India.

I never saw Nanking again.

Section II

American Interlude

Chapter 1
Sunnyslope

THE WHITE FRAME FARMHOUSE has stood for well over a hundred years on this gentle slope facing the south. The early Quakers who settled Morrow County, Ohio, had an eye for good sites for their homes, and the Benedicts who first came here were particularly fortunate in their choice.

The house sits a quarter of a mile back from the country road to the east and about the same distance from an intersecting road to the north, which is no longer in use. At the end of East Lane stands a mailbox keeping the lines of communication with the outside world open throughout the generations for those who lived up at the house known far and wide by the appropriate name of *Sunnyslope.*

The box has safely kept within its bosom letters and seed catalogs, bills no doubt, the *Ohio Farmer, Morrow County Independent*, and other papers; Montgomery Ward's catalog was the department store visited with much enjoyment from a rocking chair, where housewives and farmers alike shopped for the needs of family and farm.

It was, however, the letters, especially letters with foreign stamps, that set the mailbox apart, for these Quakers were in touch with the far corners of the earth. The old mailbox, covered with a blanket of snow at this moment, has held within it the strangest mail of any mailbox for miles around.

Letters from China, letters from India, letters from the islands of the sea, and from the countries of Europe, South America, and Africa as well.

The letters in the mailbox had a great deal to do with the character of the house. Of course, it should have been said the other way about, as the character and worldwide interests of the people at the house determined the letters that filled the box at the end of the lane, but one of those letters changed not only the character and future of the old house on the hill but mine as well.

The house lies empty now—and the mailbox is resting. Who knows when the international letters will flow into it again! For a week I have returned after fifty years, to warm myself at the old fireplace where I sat as a child. I sit in Grandma Lizzie's chair rocking a little as I used to see her do, beside the table where Aunt Martha sat to write letters and which I dusted every Saturday. I must say it looks fifty years older now, as also do the other original pieces of furniture that are left.

Through the window down toward the mailbox from my chair here near the fire, the countryside looks just as it did fifty years ago. The fields are covered with snow, and the trees, which were iced with silver branches yesterday, have an extra coat of freshly fallen snow. I could be looking at a Currier-Ives picture —one of their finest—but this is no Christmas card. It is my girlhood home. The pine trees I see are showing their age. Like the people, most of them are gone, and the few who remain stand out in the snow close together holding each other up—or are they just leaning against one another for comfort in this storm?

The house stands halfway between two lanes, as I have said, but it also stands halfway between the nearest towns. One gives it a post office address; the other town provides the school. They are both three miles away. In my day, we counted on an hour to go to town by horse and buggy. Today it is just a matter of minutes to either. The towns have changed as towns do in fifty years, but today under the blanket of snow, the farm, the lane, the house, the barn, the chicken house, the woods—they all look as they always have on a winter's day—and the scene is very beautiful, very rural American.

The big white barn has a date written on it—1854. That was when the Benedict family took residence here in this lovely spot. Elbert Benedict was the first Benedict I knew. He and his wife, Martha Wood Benedict, lived here for many years. He was a progressive farmer and had one of the best farms in the country. His wife was a very large woman, and a very hard-working one.

There had been a corn-drying factory nearby once, and she managed the cooking for sixty and more young people who came to work during the corn-drying season. The long dining table was filled three times at each meal, and she kept a bustling household, overseeing every department of work at the house. The boys slept in tents, and she managed a rather large dormitory for girls as well.

There were no children in this home, but all the young folk for miles around called Martha Benedict "Aunt Martha." She kept a lifelong interest in the young people who worked for her and had a profound influence on the whole community.

Uncle Elbert and Aunt Martha were deeply spiritual. They were Quakers from way back, and their ancestors were among those who settled this area, giving the community growing up on both banks of Alum Creek the name of Quakertown. They were active in the Quaker meeting—never missed a service. They were known as "weighty Friends," which meant they were on the important boards and committees of the church—influential members. Theirs was an open home to visiting Friends and at quarterly meeting time; when other houses were snowbound or mudbound, this house was always accessible, and it was quite usual to entertain as many as 24 to 30 guests overnight. They were equipped for large crowds.

Missions was one of the special interests of this unusual couple. For many years Uncle Elbert was treasurer of the Ohio Friends Mission Board. Aunt Martha loved to entertain missionaries in her home, and thus guests from India, China, and other countries not only came for a visit but often made it a recuperation center. Each one left a gift from her own part of the

Orient, and in time a whole bookcase of three sections was filled with artifacts from around the world. They are still here locked in their places as they were years ago when I was given the job of keeping them dusted and in order.

One day a letter from Sunnyslope came to my mother that changed everything for Benedicts, for all of us, and for the farm itself.

We were in China then. Father had just died, and Mother was ill. It was obvious that we would have to come home. And then the letter came from the Benedicts at Sunnyslope inviting Mother and the three of us to make Sunnyslope our home until Mother was able to return to China.

The day the letter of invitation came to Mother in faraway China was a happy one for her. She was ill and had to return to America widowed and with three children—but where? Where was there room for all of us? The letter from the box at the end of the lane at Sunnyslope was the answer—a perfect one. There was a farm with work to do, open spaces, good food and loving care, and willing hands to help. Temporarily anyway—it was perfect.

Thus Sunnyslope became a halfway house for our youth, standing between China and our childhood there and college in America.

And so it was that Sunnyslope became our home.

Aunt Martha was a cripple in two ways, and the one aggravated the other. She was very large—the largest woman I think I have ever seen. She also had broken her ankle while papering the dining room. The ankle never quite healed—at least not enough to support her weight; and so she sat to do all her work, which in turn made it almost impossible for her to get the exercise she needed where she needed it the most. She was a tremendous burden to herself at times and suffered constantly, but, nothing daunted, she worked the whole day through—baking, stirring, peeling, churning, canning. Her work was with her hands and arms while she sat on a reinforced high chair beside the wood-burning stove producing the most delicious food one could ever hope to taste.

Her heart was as much bigger than the usual heart as her body was larger than that of the normal woman. She cared about everyone and mothered everyone who needed mothering. She whistled hymn tunes in a frantic kind of way when she was in pain, and only then did one know she was miserable, but never did she complain. But there were times when I thought, as others must have, that I wished she would complain a little and forget the whistling—but this was not Aunt Martha's way. The cheery tunes gave her strength and courage, and she always took the strong way.

Uncle Elbert was kind to Aunt Martha. He was one of the first of the Quakers in Quakertown to buy a car, making it easier for her to get around; to have an indoor bathroom, to put in a Delco plant for electricity in the house, to get an electric washing machine, though the latter was a very different contraption from what is known by that name today. It was a wooden affair, but the rubbing was taken over by machinery, and that was progress.

Uncle Elbert was temperamental. He was very enthusiastic and very, very low-spirited in turn. He was driven by an inner compulsion and hindered by "bondage" to little things that made big things out of small concerns. This was true of interpretation of Scripture and equally true of the way he insisted on mispronouncing words. To him, "deaf" was "deef"; "Psalms" was "Sams," and "surrup" was his way of saying "syrup."

He was a good farmer and more successful than many. His brother Walter lived down the road at the next farm with his wife Kate and their seven children, three boys and four girls. Aunt Martha's older sister Elizabeth lived at Sunnyslope with her. She was known as Grandma Lizzie.

At the end of the lane lived Emma Barton in an old house darkly hidden among pine trees and a mammoth cottonwood tree out in front, which gave the place the name *Cottonwood.*

Emma Barton was a little old woman from the distant past —the kind one thinks of as having always been old. Her calico dresses were to her ankles—full-skirted—and the waist buttoned down the front with tin buttons. Her long, stringy grey hair was done in an untidy knot on the top of her head. She came and went with a lantern by night—and kept an oil lamp burning on her table, which shone out dimly through the trees. Emma Barton was not a servant. She was far too independent for that. She did, however, work for Aunt Martha and spent most of every day helping with the washings, the leg work that Aunt Martha could not manage. She papered and cleaned and gardened and worked like a man, and at evening she returned to her house and lit her lamp.

I never thought to ask who she was or why she lived so aloof and alone, why she was so different in every way, like a woman who was left over from another age. We just accepted Emma Barton as she was.

The boys worked in the barn doing chores and in the fields making hay, and I worked in the house as legs for Aunt Martha. I helped Emma clean the twelve-room house every Saturday. We washed dishes in the oversized stone sink, where kettles blackened over an open wood fire made cleaning a messy job, as they had to be scrubbed with coal oil. There was something to do at every season and for every minute of the day, and I learned my first lessons in exhaustion.

I had never worked before in my life. The Chinese amah would never let me, although sometimes a womanly instinct jogged me even as a little girl into a wild desire to clean. Whatever was lying about out of place to spoil my sense of tidiness, I threw in the closet, and Mother was so pleased to come home from the hospital to a well-ordered house. She thanked me and told me what a comfort I was to her—until she opened the closet, when suddenly her mood changed. What happened was much like what happened to Fibber Magee's closet, but I knew nothing of that then.

Mother's pleasure in me changed to profound distress as we sorted the outpourings of the closet once the door was opened! I never had had occasion to be tired of work—but on the farm I became tired as I never dreamed possible, working steadily from dawn till night.

I can see Aunt Martha now sitting on the raised chair, canning fruit on a hot summer night, stirring while the sweat (for on the farm it was sweat) poured down her pleasant face.

When the day's work was done, I went out on the back porch to watch the sun glide gently down behind the wood. I leaned against the post and pondered life.

Mother was very ill and I wondered what would happen to us. Would things ever be right again for our family? I dreamed there leaning against the post; I dreamed of love, of being a doctor someday, for it had not occurred to me that any of us would not be doctors someday. It was the family tradition, and I hoped it would lead me back to China.

I thought out the hurts and bruises that frequently occurred, particularly the loneliness of being a stranger, the shame of having to learn what every farm girl knew already, the humiliation of not knowing how to play with other young people, of just knowing I was really not one of the young people in the sense of belonging.

The "leaning post" became a very necessary retreat, particularly after Mother died, for she died at Sunnyslope on just such a December day as this.

Mother had been very ill all summer long. She lay out under the trees on a cot each nice day. Aunt Martha did her best to tempt her appetite, but Mother's restrictive diet did not allow for the usual delicious Sunnyslope fare. Boiled liver or raw beef sandwiches were prescribed by the doctor.

Once during the summer we thought Mother was dying. We stood around her bed and sang. She kept quoting the 27th Psalm, and then she fell asleep. The family thought it was the end, but the doctor came and said she was sleeping naturally and restfully for the first time. When she awoke, she seemed better, much better. She soon was able to be about again and help with peeling apples and shelling peas. By September she was better than she had been in eighteen years, and we began to make plans to return to China the following fall.

Mother began to speak at missionary meetings again. In late November she went south for deputation work. She returned early in December, and in ten days she was gone.

She had expressed a desire during the summer when there seemed little hope of recovery that we three should be kept together in one home. There were offers to keep one or the other of the three of us, but Mother kept hoping we would not have to be separated. When Benedicts offered to give us a home together, Mother was at peace. So now that she was gone, we learned that we three would henceforth belong to the Benedicts, that Sunnyslope was not a place to live until we returned to China; it was to be our home.

There were adjustments to be made and a loneliness that found no comfort until, after a hard day, I went to lean against my "leaning post" to think.

The thoughts were not all sad, for answers came to me out there. I saw that nothing could be better for me, who had been served all my life and spared all kinds of hard work, than the discipline of early rising and hard labor, obeying orders of one who knew how to do all manner of things that women need to know. She, though a cripple, never made an excuse of her handicap. There was no complaining, just doing what needed doing cheerfully with no alternative.

I thought of servants I had known in China who would not let me lift a finger. How hard they worked all day with nothing to make work easier: no running water, no electricity, no prepared foods. It was time I learned how to serve, to work, and what it means to have no alternative than what needed to be done. I felt better after that awareness. There was, at least, a purpose to life, even to the unpleasant part. I am glad now that I sensed that then and that my leaning post reveries brought not only comfort but good sense as well.

Soul-searching frequently occupied my back porch thinking. A great deal of stress was put upon modest dress, and modesty was measured in those days by fractions of inches. Regular attendance at church and all church-established functions was imperative. There were no acceptable reasons why one stayed away except for real illness. There were many strict outward regulations, and at the Benedict house, we went all the way.

I could never be sure I did what I did because I must or because of personal convictions. My older brother and I were expected, on occasion, to speak on China and eventually even take the Sunday morning worship service. I did not doubt my brother's sincerity. His "leaning post" was down at the barn, and whatever else he did there I do not know, but that he prayed there I was sure, as he prayed out loud so that one could hear him up at the house; and no one questioned the sincerity of his prayers. He was most unusually conscientious, and I was very sensitive, but just an ordinary girl with ordinary feelings and reactions who often compared unfavorably with Charles.

There was much to ponder, to relinquish, to regret, and to be desired; and I too talked to God in a very practical way. Mother always did. Her prayers were direct and childlike, and she prayed as though she expected help and answers in detail. I am so glad I knew then what Mother did about her problems.

Sitting here tonight, so many years later, I wonder if perhaps this farm, this loneliness, this sense of need for help from outside myself as a girl, as well as the dependence, the introduction to the hard knocks of life, and the discipline were not perhaps the best moments of all.

If life then were an uninterrupted, unclouded, normal childhood, would I have needed the leaning post? Do we really find help unless we know we need it? Do we light a light unless we sense darkness? Do we take by childlike faith that for which we sense no longing?

Ezra attended the local one-room schoolhouse with a Quaker man for a teacher. That was something I always wanted to do, but Charles and I were old enough to have to drive Midget, the mare, to Ashley to school each day—three miles each way. They have a school bus now, and the country school is no more, and I have no regret for the passing of the horse-and-buggy stage!

Chapter 2
Life on the Farm

AT SUNNYSLOPE, AFTER SCHOOL, there was work waiting. We put up hundreds of jars of fruit and vegetables. We dried corn. We rendered lard and packed sausage into jars to pressure cook. We made pickles, and at the end of the season, we made more pickles out of whatever was left in the garden.

Washday was something in those days. We began by sorting on the dining room floor; we boiled the white clothes on the kitchen stove, carried pails of hot clothes to the dank basement, where there was a motor-driven washer and electric wringer. Clothes were brought back up in large wicker baskets and hung out on the line in the beautiful yard among the trees crippled with age. In the winter the clothes were hung over the register in the living room on a clothes rack, and the house filled with steam.

When there were eggs, there were hundreds of eggs to clean and pack. When we had milk, there were gallons to separate, separator to wash, cream to churn into butter. When we had strawberries, we picked them by the bushel and sorted them for sale. We did things in a big way at this house, and I have thought since how good it was that Uncle Elbert did not get all his big ideas at once!

As I discovered, there were few moments to waste.

The guardians who kept us and gave us a home have long since died. The farm now belongs to my brothers, who are seldom in America, as both are missionaries; but this is where they come when furlough time comes around. And I come to visit now and then even when they are not here, for it is home to me, too, in a way.

The paper on the walls in some of the rooms—mine, I'm sure—is the original paper. But when papering is done as it was last summer in the front rooms—I was here and helped scrape off the old—it seemed to me the paper came off in decades, the brown scrolls, the dark green, floral roses, and more recently lighter shades. There has been a lot of living in this house, a lot of hard work, a lot of generosity and caring for others—the sick, missionaries on furlough, orphaned children who otherwise would have been separated with one here and one there. There have been quarterly meeting guests to feed, farmhands, thrashers, evangelists, and visitors.

This house is spelled by the letters that say "hospitality" in a day when everything was work. I too learned to work, not when I felt like it, but work regardless, and I learned about hospitality. It was not something you did to show off your new rug or curtains or to show off your cooking. It was a ministry for the Lord, a service to His people because they had need of you.

My mother's home had been a hospitable home. She had opened her home to all kinds of guests. I felt at home with all kinds of people—but—Mother had the servant do the work while she worked all day in the hospital. Here I was the servant! Ah, this was different, but even then I knew deep within me that I needed to know the true cost of what doing for others meant, and later I was glad for the training at Sunnyslope, for I too was destined to have an open home both with and without help.

Meals were tremendous in both amounts and variety. There was meat from the farm, fresh or cooked and canned on the basement shelves. Vegetables from the garden or canned were our own. There was nearly everything—milk, cream, butter, and cottage cheese. Why do not people today make cottage cheese like Aunt Martha used to make! Is it really a lost art? In any case there was no need for skimpy meals. I never dreamed one could cook without cream and that rice pudding could be made in smaller amounts! I still cook too much. Aunt

Martha gets into me now and then, and I "cook up a storm." but Aunt Martha's spirit is hard to find today. Is hospitality really a thing of the past in America?

One summer our dear, dear Auntie Holme from China came to the farm, and she and I were roommates all summer. She was in and out, of course, but after her missionary deputation stints, she came back to my room and shared it with me. What a wonderful privilege that was! Mother was gone and I poured out to her hours of girl talk, my first flutters of love, my hopes and fears; and she brought me up-to-date on what had happened in China. She gave her blessing to the young lad who has now become my husband. If Auntie Holme approved, then I was on safe ground; she did, and I was!

The Williams family also were frequent visitors at Sunnyslope. They were relatives in some distant kind of way with Benedicts, as we were in another way. When Walter Williams came, it was like having Father. There were just the two men in the China days, and this family was closer than any blood relationships to me except my brothers. Walter Junior had two brothers when they came back to America, both born in China after we left.

The frequent contact with China folk was a great lift to me and made me feel like a whole person. Sometimes children who live one life and suddenly an entirely different life, particularly if some kind of trauma or loss is involved, need a little contact with the former to keep from feeling torn in two.

Uncle Elbert felt keenly as a member of the missionary board the responsibility to see that nothing would stand in the way of each of the three of us going to China as missionaries. Certainly no young lad was to turn my head from the course I had set for myself—which was to result in my being a medical doctor to China.

In Mother's dying moments, she sat up and cried out, "Who will go?" Charles and I were in the room and we knelt beside her bed and each said, "I will, Mother." What Mother saw or where she meant us to go, we did not really know, but I was sure she meant China, and so was Uncle Elbert sure, and everyone else eventually understood that Charles and I had promised Mother on her deathbed that we would go to China.

Thus when lads who were not committed to being a missionary to China wrote to me, the letters were censored and sometimes I never saw the letter, only the envelope. The boys figured I did not like them and thought myself too good to write, which added considerably to the feeling of loneliness. China was far away, and my need for companionship was a very immediate one.

There was never the relaxed sense of living day by day and waiting to see how God would lead. The future was rigidly set, and I was in great bondage to it and also in bondage in my life as a Christian.

I wrote in my diary religiously every night, and something of that sixteen-year-old pressure hits me now as I read its pages.

My high school years were not happy ones. Spiritually I had very exaggerated ideas of what God expected of me. Often on weekends, Charles and I spoke at missionary meetings, took Sunday services, and did all kinds of grown-up things while Uncle Elbert drove us about in his Ford, managing our appearances. During the week I felt condemned for the slightest failure. I lived in fear of grieving the Lord. There was nothing natural or winsome about the bondage under which I struggled. Uncle Elbert was extreme in many of his own views and lived in somewhat of a strain himself.

He and Aunt Martha had bravely undertaken a frightening responsibility. Not only had they never had any children, but they could not have found a stranger set of three children to bring up. Outdoor work on the farm was not so difficult, as the boys loved the farm; but in the housework with Aunt Martha—a strictly "business" type—the East and West had quite a bit of adjusting to do! Furthermore, the eyes of the whole denomination not only were on us children but on them. How were they doing with their undertaking? Were they turning us out to be the missionaries that we were expected to be? Were they strict enough? It must have been a terrific strain for them. It was for me!

Grandma Lizzie had a room upstairs opposite mine. No one but the two of us knew the nights I slipped into her room.

She was a very loving and understanding person and knew the comforting things to say, and she said them.

I have thought a great deal about the people in our lives—the ones who demand our best and build fiber and character in us, the ones who pressure us beyond our true ability, those who speak comfortably to us and are able to understand without words, with whom we can be completely ourselves. I feel sometimes we could do with more of the comforting variety—life being what it is for most of us. And yet I am thankful for rigid guidelines. With all our moving back and forth from one culture to another, we were never lost with Aunt Martha, with whom one felt perfectly safe and even solid.

Chapter 3

Following a Dream

CHARLES AND I WENT TO Ashley School three miles away, anyway you look at it, and we looked at it from a horse and buggy in all kinds of weather, hurrying back each night to help with the work on the farm. We took the milk and eggs into town to be sold and dragged another buggy behind ours to be repaired when necessary. We kept Midget, Grandma Lizzie's horse, in the barn belonging to the high school principal during the day, feeding her at noon.

When Charles was with me, he did the hard things, everything like hitching up and tending to Midget, doing farm errands; but I was two years behind him, and the two years left over after he graduated for me to drive alone looked bleak indeed. I had never been without Charles, and now that our parents were gone, I could not bear the thought of two years without him.

A committee had been appointed by my mother to supervise our college education, and the Sunday schools of Ohio Yearly Meeting of Friends made it their project to put us through college financially. The time came when Charles went to Marion College, in Marion, Indiana, leaving me behind. It was our first year of separation, and I doubled my efforts to follow him in the shortest possible time; the following September came none too soon for me to join him at Marion.

Ezra attended a one-room country school close by. He loved to farm and was happiest when he was there with Aunt

Martha. He was reluctant to accompany Charles and me when we attended missionary meetings, especially when the "DeVol children" were expected to speak, as was frequently the case. The one thing he did not want to do was to be a missionary when he grew up, and he avoided identification with anything that pointed in that direction.

And, yet, it was he whom God did call specifically to become a medical missionary, and he *did* go to China and followed more closely than either Charles or me in our parents' footsteps. He did not have to shed, as I did, the phony compulsion to fulfill my parents' lifework.

Once in college, I took all the premedical subjects I could squeeze into my schedule. I loved every minute of college life. There we were no longer special in any way. We rose or fell on our own reputation, and no one was concerned with our past lives or future plans. The Yearly Meeting came through with our necessary expenses, for which we had to give an accurate accounting of every detail.

It was understood at Sunnyslope that since we were being supported, there would be no wasteful expense of any kind—no candy, no extras, no clothing without permission.

Aunt Martha said she got married with one good dress and one everyday one, and she doubted if I would need many clothes. Many a night I stayed in my room rather than venture out in the unsuitable clothes I did have until the idea of borrowing struck me as a great possibility, but it did not strike anyone else as such a good idea—particularly my roommate!

It was during my junior year that I began to wonder about how much of me was real, how much was a concession to those who supported me, and how much was my own desire to turn out as a medical missionary to China.

Charles was married the summer of that year to a college friend, Leora Van Mater. The missionary board members were invited to the wedding, as well as the New York relatives and all the friends round about in Quakerdom and Quakertown, as well as college friends. The wedding was at Alum Creek Friends Church and the reception at Sunnyslope. Aunt Martha was flat on her back with sciatica rheumatism, and I was both bridesmaid and hostess for the houseful of overnight guests as well as for the reception; my thoughts were ones of longing when there was a moment to lean against the post on the back porch after all the excitement was over.

Charles and Leora really *were* going to China immediately. There was no more leaning on Charles. His dreams had come true.

I was keeping company with Everett Cattell, a Quaker lad, also attending Marion College. His mother was on the missionary board.

He wanted to be a missionary to China for my sake, but never having had a call, he would not claim one. He seemed so right for me in every way except for that one thing—and yet I felt that surely we would eventually go together to China just as Charles and Leora were about to do.

We were so sure about each other that Everett came to Sunnyslope that summer and asked Uncle Elbert for permission for us to become engaged.

The two of them sat on the swing on the front porch and talked until very late, and the answer was NO. Uncle Elbert said, "Nothing but failing health or disobedience to God could keep Catherine from China." If Everett was not sure of his call, there was no use in pursuing even the friendship as he saw it.

The question of my call to China did not even *then* arise. I had lived in the dream so long that I never doubted that it was God's will.

In the fall of my last year at Marion, Leora's mother challenged my call one evening after a soul-searching sermon.

"Tell me about your call," she ventured. "Frankly, I doubt that you have one. You impress me as a girl who is following a dream. Sure, your parents were doctors. Sure, you want to go back to China, but did God ever really tell you to go there?"

These were hard words. They upset my whole reason for being, for trying so hard; but very late that night I agreed to disengage myself from all China plans. I would write the board,

Uncle Elbert, and all who were involved in the China aspect of my life. I would settle down to live in America like any other American girl, with no special exotic plans, and let God call me or not call me, as He willed.

It was a dying such as I had never experienced. My decision was accepted by those to whom I wrote and welcomed by some who had suspected that only my homesickness for China had constituted the call. That Charles had really gone and I could no longer plan to go to China was a traumatic blow; I wept for days with a feeling of total emptiness and lostness. My eyes were also failing, and doctors had already told me that the study of medicine with its demand for greater strain—looking in microscopes—was impossible for me. And thus my plans crashed about me.

In the last year of college I could not change my major and prepare for some other line of work, but neither was there any further barrier to our engagement, so we planned to be married in August after graduation. I dreamed of a church wedding with all my Quakertown, Quakerdom, college friends, and board members. And Walter Williams, who was still Uncle Walter to me, would marry us.

But this was not to be.

After going through college on the very smallest of wardrobes, suddenly at graduation a dear cousin in New York who owned a clothing store sent me a beautiful coat trimmed in white fur, several dresses, and dainty underthings. I was rich. Besides this I had a beautiful white Chinese silk brocade that Auntie Holme had given me for a graduation present. I felt ready for marriage with the trousseau all provided. Altogether, and for the first time in my life, I had ten dresses!

Six weeks before the wedding, Aunt Martha agreed to let me visit Everett's family in Alliance, Ohio. I had never been in their home, so it was arranged; I was to take the train to Alliance, where Everett was to meet me.

The new dresses and pretty things were packed with utmost care in a round hatbox-like suitcase that Everett had given me for Christmas.

Going on deputation with "Uncle Elbert" after mother's death.

Mother and we children going on deputation in Ohio after father's death.

Sunnyslope house and barn

Catherine

College scientists Catherine and Achash Endsley

At Marion College (Charles, Catherine, and Ezra)

Catherine meets Everett Cattell.

Wedding Day

Helen Jackson,
Catherine, Everett,
John Leedy, son of President
of Marion College,
Samuel Mosher,
Y.M. Supt. of Ohio

Wedding guests at Sunnyslope

Pastor and family, First Friends,
Cleveland, Ohio
(Everett, Catherine and David Cattell)

S. S. Tampa sailing Sept. 4, 1936 - New York for Bombay. Evangeline Stanley, Barbara Ann, Catherine, David, Chester Stanley, Everett. Off to India.

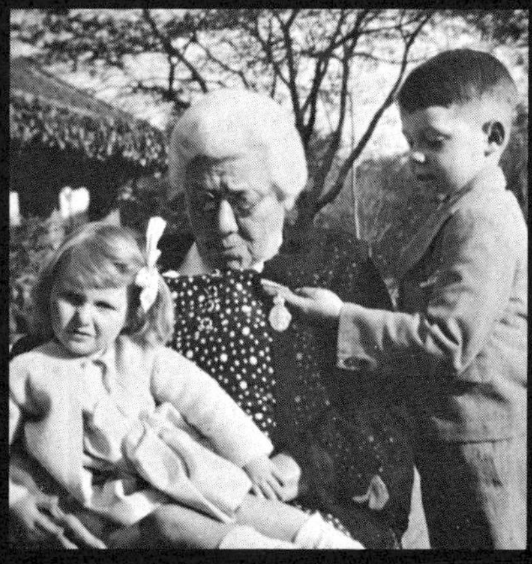

Esther Baird with David and Barbara looking at medal.

Nowgong household with Miss Baird and her medal.

Catherine and Everett Cattell

Barbara, David

Patsy Ann Cross and Barbara carried to school.

We had a delightful week together meeting Everett's friends and getting acquainted with his family. We made our final plans for the wedding, and Everett's mother made the wedding dress of white georgette.

It was further arranged that I would spend another ten days at Mt. Pleasant, where Elizabeth Jenkins lived in a gracious home on top of the hill. Elizabeth Jenkins was appointed one of our educational guardians by Mother shortly before her death. She had been president of the missionary board and had visited China when I was two years old. She was a Quaker lady from a prominent family of Quakers and was highly respected and much loved. It was a great honor to be her guest.

Auntie Oliver, who had been such a favorite auntie in China, also lived with Elizabeth Jenkins (known as Miss Lily in her community, but known to us as Auntie Jenkins). It was such a joy to have this time with these two, who were also very favorable to the coming marriage.

I repacked my precious belongings, and Everett put me on the train for Dillonvale, where Auntie Jenkins was to meet me.

It was the Fourth of July and the hour was noon. The train stopped. I got off. There was not a soul in sight except the one gentleman who got off also. I looked for the car from Mt. Pleasant, for Auntie Jenkins and her chauffeur. The town was empty. How was I to get to Mt. Pleasant? I went to inquire in the store and found it closed, but a lady from within told me that the whole town was out at a Fourth of July celebration. There were no taxis, no one going to Mt. Pleasant. She was sorry she could not help me.

The stranger overheard her remark and ventured, "I happen to be going to Mt. Pleasant; I have a car here; could I be of any assistance?"

"Oh, how very kind!" I replied eagerly, "I was expecting to be met here, but no one came."

"Hop in," he said pleasantly. So, suitcase in hand, I hopped into his car.

We had scarcely started when Elizabeth Jenkins drove into town with a woman who came to sell eggs. She saw me in a stranger's car, "going off with a strange man!"

I got out of the car with some stammering explanation that "this is the lady whom I was expecting," and thanked the stranger.

"Doesn't thee know not to get in cars with strange men? Doesn't thee know that if I say I will meet thee, that I will meet thee? We had car trouble, and this friend brought me. Now, thee get in with us." (It was a Model T Ford coupe.) "There are eggs in the back, so thy case must ride on the running board. I am shocked at thy going off with that man."

I must have tried to explain, but my explanation was unacceptable. I had taken a terrible risk, and it was the only topic of conversation as we climbed the steep grade to Mt. Pleasant.

After some time, I looked to see if the suitcase was all right—it was gone! The car was stopped. We got out. We looked everywhere, down the mountain—walking back looking into the valley below. The suitcase was gone! Gone were all my dresses—all the treasures that had been so recently received—the clothes that were to see me through a wedding and the life of a pastor's wife so soon to begin!—all except the Chinese silk which I had left at home.

We advertised—we offered rewards—we organized a search party. The suitcase was gone for good.

The ten days were spent sewing, making new clothes. The missionary society made me a dress, Auntie Jenkins bought me one, and I was down again to two dresses beside the one I wore!

Auntie Oliver had her teeth pulled during the ten days, so she was not quite her jolly self, but it was most comforting to have her near. She was always one to be on my side, and I needed some approval, although I do agree I needed the lecture. I also could do with a bit of healing ointment, of which Auntie Oliver had so much for sore spirits.

I spent a good deal of time making the list of 200 guests for the wedding. When Uncle Elbert and Aunt Martha came to get me and take me home, Uncle Elbert gave me $25 for the wedding to get "what I needed." I was further told they had already made out the list of wedding guests and there would be no big wedding but a small one at the house with the family and a few friends whom they would choose, which included no board members, and I was cut off from the missionary world of which I was so much a part. The Williamses were not invited, nor were many others I wanted so much. The fact that I was not a missionary candidate was a terrible blow to the Benedicts, and few understood why we had such a quiet home wedding.

Auntie Oliver was there and decorated the archway with clematis for me; Elizabeth Jenkins was there; the Benedicts and a few of my friends from Quakerdom; and college friends. There were thirty in all, including Everett's family.

We took a pastorate in Columbus, Ohio, and for nine years there was little hope of missionary work anywhere outside of Ohio.

It was the end of our Sunnyslope days and the beginning of life of the church as well as its problems—American style.

It should be said that Charles and Leora were at our wedding. They not only had been to China in the year but returned back to Sunnyslope in time for our marriage. They went out full with their lovely wedding gifts and belongings to last six years. They came back empty, having lost everything and escaping barely with their lives. In March of their first wonderful year of marriage and of China, the Nanking Incident took place, when there was such massacre, such looting and hunting down of all foreigners, that to escape with life was indeed a miracle.

Everett and I left in his Model T Ford for our honeymoon in Michigan, with Uncle Elbert holding the hose on anyone attempting to play pranks on our getaway.

I left behind me that day the life at the halfway house—Sunnyslope—to begin a new life—with Everett, my gifted and wonderful new husband, in a parsonage.

In retrospect one can see far more clearly the necessary part of those priceless years of generous, loving, protective, and faithful sharing that a couple had to offer to three orphaned children in a strange land, and I wish now there were some way to thank all the Benedicts living and dead for moving over to make room for us who so unexpectedly invaded their lives and homes and altered their pattern of living.

The mailbox lies empty now, but come furlough time for my brothers, the letters from faraway places will come to it again.

Chapter 4

Following the Plan

OUR FIRST HOME WAS the parsonage in Columbus. It was a little house. It was empty and we had very little with which to furnish it. We had a bed, a kitchen table, a rocking chair, a rug for the living room, and a sewing machine. We moved into the house on Wednesday morning, bringing only a pail, mop, broom, and cleaning equipment, wearing old clothes. Our belongings were being brought by a friend later in the day by truck.

Prayer meeting time came and still our clothing and bedding and wedding gifts had not arrived. We were in our work clothes, soiled now by the day's scrubbing. The white brocade silk dress had been put into the car the last minute as we were leaving Sunnyslope, so I had that; but it matched very poorly with old shoes and the rest of our attire. The dress was inappropriate for prayer meeting, as the rest of us was unsuitable in the other direction of shabbiness. But we were expected at prayer meeting, and it had been announced that the bride would be present and members urged to come and meet her!

We were there in our finery and in our rags at one and the same time. How we managed to live that first impression down I'll never know, but the people were kind. And one couple understood, for they invited us to spend the night with them and until our things arrived, which was a great step in the direction of becoming lasting friends.

We were there in the first pastorate three years. During that time Everett got his master's degree at Ohio State, and we had become adjusted to the life and work of the city church.

During those years we had guests constantly passing through our humble home—missionaries of many countries, evangelists, students, college friends, and quarterly meeting guests.

I started out cooking like Aunt Martha with butter and cream, but soon learned that food could be cooked in a less expensive manner.

We had our first garden and harvested a crop of marbles instead of potatoes, but we ate them and pretended that they were a special kind of delicacy.

We were asked then to take an extension church in Springfield. We lived in the Lutheran Missionary Home, and our church was a garage with unpainted platform and benches. That was a challenge indeed to surpass all challenges! How to make people want to attend a garage to worship was a real problem.

David was born that year, and Auntie Williams came to stay with me the ten days before David arrived. She said that my mother had helped her in her hour in China, and since Mother was gone, she wanted to be with me in my hour. To me, the days with her in the home were most precious, and we relived our China days together and prepared for the advent of our firstborn.

David was a beautiful boy—dark auburn hair, brown eyes, a strong and bright, happy baby.

Charles was teaching at Marion College during this time, and their first child was born a few months before David's birth. Their daughter Margaret was named for our dear Margaret Holme.

Ezra was a junior at Marion, and he had his own ambitions and personal plans, which decidedly did not include being a missionary or a doctor; but it was in this year that suddenly he came face to face with God's call—and if he went God's way he knew exactly what it would mean. God had called him to be a missionary doctor, and China was the field. It was he, not I, who was to return to the work left so long ago by our parents.

About the time of Ezra's experience with God—when he put the whole matter of finance, getting into a medical school, and all other impossibilities into God's hands—everything began to work out, not only for him but for us.

Everett was asked to go to Cleveland to be pastor of First Friends Church there and to teach part time at Cleveland Bible Institute. Ezra was accepted at Western Reserve Medical School, where only 78 out of 700 applications were accepted.

We felt led to go there and at the same time make a home for Ezra, helping with room, board, and what expenses we could manage.

For four years, while we served both church and school, Ezra lived with us. They were years of miracles as we watched God do the impossible for Ezra time after time, meeting his needs, healing his body, helping him in his studies, passing exams, winning favor of the hostile. These were days of the depression. Money was scarce. Our well-to-do parishioners became poor overnight. Traumas of a serious nature were experienced by most of our members. And yet we were able to move the church from what had become the red-light district of Cleveland to a more suitable part of the city, and God's work went on.

During December of our fifth year at Cleveland, Barbara Anne was born. David was five. He was dismally disappointed. This "playmate" he had been waiting for was to have been a boy, and anyhow the baby was too little for a playmate.

He was a bit hostile about his disappointment and was very mischievous anyway; during his fifth year he managed to get the house on fire twice. No great damage was done, except to the living room rug, over which I threw a pan of starch that happened to be in my hand when I saw the blaze! The next time the davenport smoldered for some time before the fire finally gave up.

Our years at Cleveland were wonderful years. We could have gone on there forever, we thought.

But one night word came of a crisis in India. The work there was threatened with possible complete shutdown. Five missionaries had resigned at one time. There was a plea for a couple who would be willing to go and start work in a new village where property had been bought. "Who will go?"

My husband announced the situation at the New Year's Eve meeting. We were to pray for a couple who would be willing to go. He was making a fervent plea.

India was out of the question as far as either of us was concerned: for him because he thought I would not consider it, and for me because I thought if God wanted us anywhere, it would be China, and since I had to give that up, missions were out.

The thought bothered me considerably, hearing my husband plead for a couple. "If it were only China," I thought.

Then, "I wish Everett wouldn't press this so about India. I hate to have him ask others to do something we are not prepared to do."

One day I heard Everett asking questions of a missionary from India. He opened up all kinds of areas for questioning. What kind of workers were most needed? How large was the area? Had there been converts? What was the political situation? I felt a little uneasy as I began to realize that he was doing some serious thinking.

India pressed upon us both. The need was urgent. The field was to be closed if someone did not volunteer. Why could we not throw off this uneasiness? Did God want us to consider it? I did some more dying during that time. We never discussed India between ourselves, but India was there between us.

At Easter time, the subject came into the open.

"I've been thinking about India a lot lately," said my husband.

"Yes, I know. I have, too."

"You have? Why, I was afraid you would not want to consider it."

"I don't, but I have been doing it anyway."

"I wonder if God wants us to offer to go," he ventured.

"I know. I wonder, too."

After the subject was in the open, we could think of nothing else.

When we were very, very sure that God had called us to go to India, we started out one afternoon to see Uncle Walter Williams, who had just returned from both China and India and had made recommendations to the board regarding work on both fields. It was he who made the call for a couple for India.

We drove along talking very little, each wondering how to offer ourselves for India. What would Walter Williams think of our going to India instead of China?

Suddenly a thought came to me. Five missionaries had resigned. No man had ever gone back to do a second term in our India mission. It was a hard field. What made us think we would succeed? What were we thinking of?

I expressed this feeling to Everett, and he said he was thinking the same thing. The more we thought about it, the more presumptuous it seemed for us to offer ourselves to the board.

"Let us go home," we said. "If God wants us to go to India, let Him suggest our names to the board. That would be a confirmation." That is what we did.

During the waiting that followed, spiritually minded people said strange things to us.

"Don't be afraid to step out if God is calling."

How did they know? We had told no one.

Then again, "Whatsoever he saith unto you, do it."

It was early June when the full board met in Damascus. On the very first night of the board meeting, there was a telephone call from them.

"Everett, would you consider going to India as our missionary? We decided tonight that if you and Catherine will go, we will give India another chance."

"Yes, we will go," came Everett's unexpected answer.

"Well, what will Catherine think about this?"

"She is ready to go."

"Don't you want to think this over?"

"No—we have been thinking it over for months. This was the fleece: that you call *us*."

The next morning we were in Damascus and under appointment to go to India in September.

It remained to tell Everett's mother, widowed by this time—and the depression had taken all she had, even her home. We stopped to tell her of the board decision on our way home. All her adult life she had been pushing missions. Everett was as much brought up in a missionary home as I had been. But our leaving her and going out for six and a half years was a hurdle both for her and for us. Everett was the eldest, and it was not easy for him, nor for her.

Donovan, the younger son, was unmarried and still at home, and he said he would care for Mother, and Mother was satisfied and came to Cleveland to help us sell our things and get ready to leave.

We did not know then, nor did she, nor did Donovan, that in one year's time he would be in heaven and Mother dependent on the girls! My husband seldom weeps. I had never seen him shed tears, but he did that night in India when he waited in prayer through the hours of night with Mother. They were the hours of the funeral and burial in Ohio.

Another hurdle was finding a pastor for our church. We had moved and Everett had taken the responsibility of the mortgage as pastor. How could we think of leaving until it was paid? The church was not happy. All kinds of reasons were expressed for our not going. The debt, the children's health (Barbara was a delicate child), the dangers of India, the need of a pastor. How could they find one on short notice? God solved that by sending Uncle Walter Williams himself; no one could have improved on that!

And so by early September, we were on a freighter headed for India—all hurdles crossed, all matters cared for, and assured of God's call and of His provision for every need.

The youth of the Yearly Meeting were touched by our going to India, and God put it on their hearts to take upon themselves our support. This they did without fail for what turned out to be nine years of our first term and eight years of our second term.

When we obey God—we have learned to expect miracles.

Section III

Mango

The Mango Tree

THE MANGO TREE BEARS its beautiful and delicious fruit in the hottest weather. When all else is dry and the hot winds blow from the burning desert, the mango tree provides a refreshing fruit at its prime.

While green, the fruit is cooked and, mixed with iced milk and sugar, becomes a drink and at the same time a tonic.

When ripe, the fleshy mango is food for a king, though abundantly available to a pauper.

The tree provides shade and there is no better spot for pitching a tent than in a mango grove. The generous leafy branches provide protection and relief from the scorching sun.

The flowers are of the sweetest fragrance, filling the night air with perfume that at times is almost too lovely to endure.

How is it that the mango tree can produce fruit so fresh, so juicy, and at the same time be the refreshing tonic, an antidote for heat stroke?

Its roots go very deep, searching for water far below the dry and arid surface. It is the depth to which it goes that makes it fruitful in adversity and fragrant and green when all else is dry and withered and barren.

Scorching winds do not discourage a mango tree. It only digs its roots deeper, searching for water; and finding it, brings up sweetness and joy from its great depths.

Winds of adversity need not rob one of lovely fruit—not if the roots go deep enough.

The mango is tonic. It is shade. It is food. It is drink. It is fragrance for rich and poor alike—available and generously giving out from the life deep within itself regardless of circumstances.

India is the land of mangoes!

Chapter 1

Land of the Mango

TAKING TWO SMALL CHILDREN to a backward native state in Central India was no small concern to us, their parents, but to many of our friends it was an unforgivable risk. I was not afraid of India, for I had learned not only not to fear China but to love China as a girl; and India was also the Orient. But I did dread the long five weeks on a freighter without a ship's doctor. If we could but get them there safely, all else seemed manageable.

There were cabin spaces for only twelve passengers, and it seemed most unlikely that comfort would be found among the few other fellow travelers. However, as the ship pulled out of New York Harbor and the twelve of us stood there to wave to dear friends who had come to see us off, we glanced shyly but curiously at one another. There we were a family of four. Beside us stood a handsome, middle-aged man with graying hair and his vivacious wife and three children, all much older than our five-year-old son and ten-month-old daughter. The gentleman spoke to us while we were still waving farewell and introduced himself as Dr. Douglas Forman, third-generation missionary to India, and a medical doctor! There was just time to shout out to our disappearing friends, "There's a doctor on board!"

The tender care and understanding love of our heavenly Father had provided the perfect traveling companions. Each day was a lesson in India culture, language, missionary problems, child care in the trying climate; and each day was fun.

As it turned out, all the fellow travelers were more at home in India than anywhere in the world, except for one businessman and our family. There was an old retired missionary—a widow of a famous educator and missionary. She was going back to beloved India to die; America wasn't fit to die in, she thought. She wanted to be among her friends—Indian friends—with whom she had lived for fifty years and more. There was a son of a missionary family, a total misfit in America who was returning to find a life in what to him was home. He was aloof, and it seemed to me a very sad commentary on what the mixing of opposite cultures can do to one, and yet to the doctor who had been born in India and his family and to the old lady (whom, by the way, I learned to love) and her missionary son, there had been no trace of damage done by transplanting from one part of the world and back again. It had broadened them into citizens of the world, where they felt at home anywhere, but with preferences, naturally.

I wondered then what makes the difference from wholesome at-homeness and total rejection of one or the other culture. This was not the last time I was to contemplate the problem, nor the cause of it.

The thirty-five days passed as the freighter plowed its way through the Atlantic, the Mediterranean and Red Sea, and on to the East and finally India, the Port of Bombay with its "Diamond Necklace" of lights curving around the shoreline of that great city. So—this is India!

We stood on deck and watched as the land of our calling drew nearer; we could see little fishing vessels dotting the harbor, the palm trees on shore, the temples, the business section, the dark faces of hundreds of coolies; as they became more and more distinct, we were each lost in his own thoughts. Out there somewhere in the center of that great land of India would be the place our children would call *home.*

The end of the long rail trip from Bombay to our Central India area was Harpalpur Station, which was the one railway station in the whole of Bundelkhand, a cluster of native states each with its Rajah, Maharajah, or Rao Sahib, according to its size and importance. They were ruled over lightly by a British political agent with headquarters in Nowgong, which was our mission headquarters as well. Thus we became, at once, guests of the British, Indian rulers, and of the people of Bundelkhand upon arrival.

The senior missionary, who was past retirement age, and the only other missionary, a nurse, Alena Calkins, met us at the railhead. The hospital was thirty-one miles on into the heart of our area, and at that time the nurse was the only missionary on the staff or in the whole city of Chhatarpur, while our senior, Miss Baird, was the only missionary in Nowgong. There had been others, but the history of the mission had been one of much coming and especially going—some by death, some for health reasons unable to return, some by just going! So with our arrival we were four adults and two small children.

Miss Calkins went back alone to her hospital, and we settled into the big red bungalow with Miss Baird, and suddenly we were missionaries—with a language to learn and a work to do and children to care for, when we ourselves were but as babes in a strange country.

When first we knew that our work was to be in India and not China, a soundless voice spoke to me so clearly I could not mistake it. I knew it was from God. "Forget the things that are behind (the emotional attachment to China, the longings, the preferences) and press forward to what is before in India. Give yourself to it. Never compare India to China."

Had someone told me that, I might not have remembered, but probably I would have said in argument, "Well, but you see . . . ." When God spoke, it was a "thus saith the Lord" to me and I never forgot.

I can see now what infinite wisdom there was in the warning. The two nations, their people, their ways were not to be judged by each other. Both were mine to love, and India was mine to serve, and for now it was India—more specifically Bundelkhand—all the way!

Our children paved the way for the happy years ahead for us, both with the British and with the Indians. Some of the time our children were the only white children in the station, and everyone made a great deal of the baby who took to Hindi first and kept her parents humping to keep up with her words and her *ayah's* words as well. The only woman we could find who could take care of Barbara over a period of time was a woman who could speak no English, and we were still in the baby stage ourselves in learning Hindi.

Kali Bai was a widow who found her way to the Methodist Hospital in Brindaban—a city of temples, a center for Hinduism, where widows gather for their daily bowl of rice in the temple. When she loses her husband, a Hindu woman loses also her place in society. She brings bad luck wherever she goes; she is no longer allowed to wear jewelry; she is reduced to a prostitute's life—the other alternative being a place at the temple to pray for the rich merchants with a bowl of rice for pay.

The prayer a widow prays is the repetition of *Ram Ram Sita Ram*. This she says over and over again, hours on end. Repetition is highly regarded not only in Hinduism but in Buddhism as well. And Kali Bai was a widow with two daughters, whom she had given to the hospital, being unable to provide for them. She herself became a Christian, and while one daughter died in an epidemic to which India is so accustomed, the other one became a graduate nurse and a beautiful Christian woman, taking further Bible school training. The mother needed work and, hearing of our need for an *ayah*, her daughter brought her to our doorstep.

She looked very much like my old *amah* in China, who had looked after the three of us when we were little. My heart went out to her and I was glad to have our baby in her care, but she had room in her heart for Barbara only. David was "Enemy No. 1" right from the first. He was left to run and find his own amusement so long as he left his baby sister alone.

Kali Bai had no idea which of the baby clothes went on first, and often after a day at language school in the mountains we were met by Kali Bai and our toddling baby; and there Barbara would be for our missionary friends to see, dressed in her strange sequence of clothing and her little undervest on the outside like a sweater!

Kali Bai learned slowly, but she loved much.

When Barbara was three, she had what was diagnosed as whooping cough three times in one year. The last time was in October when I was going to the hills to take my second year's Hindi exams. She developed pneumonia on the way up to the mountains, and I put her into the hospital even before we got to our little cottage. I was told we had arrived just in time, that the child was very ill and must be admitted, so Kali Bai and I left her there, calling out in her fright at being left in the strange place, "*Bai ji, Mamie, Bai ji, Mamie.*"

Kali Bai turned to me and gave me the worst scolding I had ever been given by an Indian: "How can you be so cruel as to leave your child among strangers?" Later I was to learn that Indian families stay at the hospital with even their adult sick. To leave a child was unthinkable. But this was an English hospital, and parents of small children were not permitted even to visit.

It was a trying time for Kali Bai and me, but eventually Barbara returned, remained thin and ill for weeks, but Kali Bai crooned over her and taught her to speak Hindi and to count in Hindi while I also was learning to speak her language.

Kali Bai's daughter, Letitia Yakub, was often able to spend her summer vacation with her mother in the hills, and I was delighted, as this splendid young nurse added confidence. I knew she was telling her mother about health matters and proper care of children. The daughter of the dear old *ayah* became an outstanding Christian worker in mid-India.

There was never any sure way of knowing, when we hired servants, just what we had done. They brought "chits" or letters of recommendation to be sure, but they borrowed them from each other, and we have had a strange assortment.

An *ayah* for one of our missionary children turned out to have leprosy. It was not at the infectious stage, but it was a shock to discover it.

One woman was a prostitute. She had the best recommendations, but they belonged to someone else.

One summer we were without a cook. We were staying down on the plains that summer, and the temperature was soaring up to 120° and more in the shade. The birds were gasping with beaks wide open, panting through the heat of the day. The water was low in the ponds and the wells. Cholera had broken out. Typhoid was common, and extra care was needed in the preparation of food and water. We had no refrigerator, and our stove was a big brick affair with holes for pots and charcoal for fuel.

We ate very late at night, about 9 o'clock, outdoors on a cement platform after the flies had gone to sleep.

We took on a local Mohammedan cook with good "chits." Eventually our dishes and silver, not to mention tins of butter from Australia that we purchased as a luxury and other food supplies, were found in the stores in the bazaars, and we were buying back our own things until finally we caught on to where the supplies were coming from—our own pantry!

One day the water carrier came to me in great distress. He said our drinking water was not being boiled. I argued with him.

"Why, I know it is being boiled every day," I said; "I go out to the kitchen every day to see that the water boils for twenty minutes."

"Yes, I know, Memsahiba, but it is the same water he boils out there every day. The water you drink comes straight from the well." And so it was. The cook told the other servants, "The memsahiba has a funny idea. She wants to see water boiling every day at 10:00 to 10:30. So I just keep the water on the stove and boil it every morning!"

The servants enjoyed telling on each other, and there were times I was grateful. Summer on the plains is a serious health hazard at best.

I often thought of the time when I was a girl in China when Tsi Si Fu and his wife took care of our home. They did all the cooking and housework. There was Lao Shih for the gatehouse and garden and Liu Da Ma for our amah, but China was not India. It did not have to contend with the caste system, where every separate work was only unto itself.

The sweeper came each day to sweep the walks and the house and clean the bathroom; the water carrier carried the water from the well; the *mali* gardened; the cook cooked, and the bearer did the dishes and waited tables; the washerman washed, taking our clothes on donkey back to the muddy ponds and bringing them back ironed. The *ayah* looked after the children; and the night watchman walked around at night clearing his throat and flashing a lantern.

Through the years we reduced the number of servants by putting in a water system and septic tanks and getting some machinery. The last two years in India we had a washing machine, and there were cooks who would wash dishes, but India is India and everyone knows his job and refuses to do another man's. The training of nurses and doctors and technicians has done much in giving a vision of Christian service that crosses all barriers of caste and caste work, but in the early days the caste system prevailed, and we were the victims. We have had all kinds of servants, but on the whole we have been most fortunate, particularly in those who had the care of our girls.

Chapter 2
Growing Roots

DAVID FOUND THE ADJUSTMENT HARD. He was old enough to remember America and not old enough to understand why we left it. In the meantime he became a great favorite with Esther Baird, our senior. My husband was put in charge immediately upon arrival because of Miss Baird's soon retirement and for other reasons. There were, or could have been, very tense times during the transfer, but David was always on the "ground floor," so to speak, with *Nani* (Grandmother), as everyone in the mission called her. If he was in mischief and expected a severe punishment, he could often be found under *Nani's* bed looking at her treasures, and she was always on his side. There were problems, but he solved as many as he made by smoothing many a rough day with his fun and antics, at which she roared with laughter.

Somewhere it should be said that a sense of humor is one of the most important of the *musts* of a missionary temperament, and I should think it would help anywhere. This we had in abundance, and it helped us all to keep our sanity.

The English found David delightful company and often invited him to the Club for tea, where all the British, both from the Agents' bungalows and from what was then Kitchener College (a school for training Indian officers), would gather. David told them all the news at the mission, which, seen through his eyes, must have been hilarious. I dreaded to have him go and would have forbidden it, but he had no playmates, and Miss

Baird encouraged the visits. He was allowed to ride the army horses with a syce running along beside with his crisp khaki turban starched to stand up high in military smartness.

David made friends with the Maharajah in the same way, and what was more to the point, he opened many a home for us with his winning and friendly chatter. Being the only white boy in the whole mission through most of his boyhood, he found his own amusement and his own friends, and made many friends for us we would not have found ourselves.

When Miss Baird was honored by the British Crown by the award of the Kaiser-i-Hind Medal just before her retirement, she was given a garden party at the Political Agent's beautiful estate. All the foreigners were invited, and those invitations were as good as commands. Everyone went. There were Indian rulers and local deputies. The garden was overflowing with officialdom. Only a handful of women were present, as Indian women did not then appear in public. We women were all in garden party hats. That, too, was a must; and I was sent in to the nearest city to buy three hats for three mission ladies to wear. So there we were, decked out in our finery, which also needed a strong sense of humor to appreciate!

Miss Baird was given her award by the highest official in our entire area, and then she was to have her picture taken with top brass and their wives. David was in the picture! Miss Baird would have it no other way, so there next to Esther Baird at her moment of high honor stood our son, who by now had turned six.

In our early years in India we lived on in the big Nowgong bungalow with most of our Christians living close by in the compound. There was an orphanage with over sixty children, who required much care, supervision, marriage arrangements, and employment; and the missionaries were responsible for them. There were several evangelists who once had been in the orphanage. They went about preaching in nearby villages, but there was need for a deeper ministry within the church and a much more intensive approach to the village work.

My husband wrestled with these problems, asking questions of the most knowledgeable, and reading books that would throw light. He looked upon problems big and little as parts of an *overall* situation. Nothing could be decided on its own merits or as an isolated problem. Every solution had to be looked at in relation to every other. A raise in salary upset the entire scale from evangelists to nurses and houseboys.

A disciplinary action had to be weighed against Indian custom, mission rules, previous action, and future trends. If one patient was too poor to pay his medical fees, then who was rich enough to pay theirs? How poor does one have to be to be exempt from fees? The overall picture had its very real and serious problems as well as its funny implications. Nearly every one in the Christian community was involved.

The tailor, carpenter, farmer, teachers, matrons, housefather, servants, gardener, nurses, compounders, and evangelists were in some way related to the orphanage, either having been brought up there or the second generation of those who had. The outreach was weak because of the ingrown nature of the church and mission impact.

We welcomed new workers and their families. Nowgong became the place where new missionaries got their start, and our family pushed on out to Chhatarpur, where the hospital was located among the Gussain tombs and where the Maharajah had finally, after twenty years, given consent for the mission to build. The mission house there was home to us and our children for seventeen years, and from this spot a half mile from town in a little house built for one single lady doctor, our work branched out in all directions.

The village work with women became my assignment—all kinds and conditions of women: our church women, the sick women in the hospital, the village women round about, the follow-up of women who had been patients, and eventually the distant women in faraway places who had not heard, and finally ministering to village women who had become Christians and needed feeding and nurturing.

In the beginning of our camping trips we took the children with us and left them in care of a half-wit. (Yes, he was an orphan, too.) He was a man of very little intelligence, but he watched the camp and peeled onions and potatoes and drew water from a nearby well and gathered wood for cooking and evening campfires. The children helped or hindered as they were inclined, and Barbara would sit squatting on her heels scouring brass cooking vessels with wood ashes and a tuft of grass roots, just like the village women.

The one "gift" the camp caretaker had was mimicry. He could mimic every missionary who ever came to that part of India. With nonsense syllables he could sound like a great preacher or tourist, serious or comic. He was so good that the whole affair was hilarious, as each of us could immediately tell who was being aped at the moment. The children loved this "ham" in him. While it certainly was not elevating companionship, neverthless the children enjoyed camplife. It was as far from the British kind of entertainment as one could imagine, but this was India, high and low, English and Indian with Americans as well, the very rich and the very poor, Christian and Hindu, from city and village, the beautiful and the hideous—all this was a part of our lives and our children's lives as well.

My husband started out as superintendent of the mission. Its planning, building, expanding, and policies—*overall* care was in his department. In the last seven years he was the executive secretary of the newly formed Evangelical Fellowship of India. This position took him away from the mission in an all-India ministry, preaching for missionary gatherings, retreats, planning conferences for pastors and evangelicals all over India.

I was still in village work, and I resented this India-wide ministry. Our family life was interrupted such a great deal as it was, but to have him gone—now to Assam, now to Burma, now to South India—it just seemed like the children would barely know their father—and I felt that we needed him at home.

One day I. Ben Wati, his assistant who was often in our home, heard me complain. I never forgot his rebuke: "Mrs. Cattell, this is not another organization. It is a movement of the Spirit of God." He was right. It has been the rallying center for spiritual renewal and evangelical witness throughout India and is even more so today with I. Ben Wati as the executive secretary, for it has grown in its ministry and reached into literature, Sunday school lessons, radio, conferences, and a ministry to pastors all over the land of India. But back in the beginning I could only see less father, less husband, and more problems, for this was the situation, and I looked at things from a mother's viewpoint.

What about the whole problem of the work versus the children and their need for parents? Already the children were in the hills nine months, much of the time in boarding school. The three months of winter when they were home were precious, but even then we had to leave them occasionally. When I went to the village for ten days at a time, the children stayed with their father, and Barbara, as she became older, learned the joys and frustrations of being hostess. Occasionally one of the India aunties kept the younger children.

Although the children were away nine months of every year after the age of six, the Plains of Central India were home.

Chapter 3

The Faith Chairs

WE HAD NO TIME TO GROW up into experienced missionaries. There we stood responsible from the beginning, but helpless as babes, unable to communicate except to a very few who knew English. It was like feeling our way in a strange and darkened room, at times guided by an Unseen Hand, and at times guided by the light that others shared with us. Two years of language study eight hours a day—and at the day's end when we could no longer learn from our books, we learned from our children who took to Hindi like ducks to water.

Then the third year threatened to destroy us and our reason for coming to India.

A simple appendectomy was considered a wise decision for my husband, who was often in villages for weeks on end with no quick transportation, or even means of communication, so he went to the nearest hospital where there was a surgeon who would undertake the routine operation. It happened to be eighty miles away in a women's hospital, and so he took a ten-day leave and I went with him, leaving the children with the new missionaries who had joined us.

Even before the operation, during the anesthetic, death grappled with his life and lost by a tiny margin, but that was only the first declaration of war. It was three months before there appeared to be any hope that he would live. I lived in the home with the missionary doctors and nurses and listened to their despair as night after night and day after day was expected to be his last. On Saturday night he would take a turn for the better only to have a new complication develop on Sunday morning.

"How will we get his body back across the river? No Indian boatman would ferry a corpse on his boat. No train would carry one. He will just have to be buried here," said the nurse; and then someone would notice me and suddenly the conversation was changed.

The emergency was a great strain on the women's mission. Another mission offered a nurse, and a British surgeon was called in for consultation. It was the day before miracle drugs and one looked only to God for miracles.

Living with the women who were fighting not only for my husband's life, but for a hospital full of patients, was not a comforting experience. We hid our concerns as best we could from each other, and much of the day and all night I was alone beside my husband or in my room.

Very late one night I heard voices, and I knew a consultation had been called, and I knew it was for Everett and an emergency. On my knees I prayed. I prayed for the life of my husband. What could I do in India left with two children to support? I needed him. Then I remembered years before my mother had been left in China to run a hospital alone, and she had three children.

I then changed the argument before the Lord.

"The children need a father. Please, oh, please, for their sakes, heal him."

But there were those hard facts again. Had we not needed a father, and were we not left without either father or mother? There are far too many orphaned children in the world to ask for special favors.

"All right, Lord," I said, "You called us here. There is no doubt about that. Even if he doesn't live, I still know You called us here. Save him for the work's sake. Surely You need him here and surely he is needed for work You called him to do."

But there again the memory of Father—the only surgeon in the whole area of China taken at the age of 46 just when he seemed to be indispensable.

Who knows where God needs us most? Who is to say what and whom God needs?

After hours of wrestling, I relinquished my husband and gave him to God and rested the entire matter in His hands. The Bible was open, and my eyes fell on the verse, "With long life will I satisfy him and shew him my salvation."

I took the entire verse. It meant what it said, and I knew not only that he would get well but also that God would show him what he could never otherwise know about His salvation and how to share it.

The next day matters were worse. The heat had settled in and was causing further complications. As I walked across the dry burning compound at midday to read the verses to him although I knew he was not conscious, I met the doctor in charge coming back for lunch, and she was weeping.

"If I lose this case, I'll never practice again," she said. "And I think I am losing it!"

"No," I said. "It is all right. I have a verse."

"Hang on to it," she said, "that is all the hope there is."

"Do you know what just happened?" I queried. "Just now a peddler came along with two wicker chairs on his head. I was needing something concrete to give strength to my faith, so I bought them both and they are on the verandah. Everett will sit in one and I will sit beside him in the other. That's a promise."

They were called the faith chairs and served as a constant reminder that this too would pass and victory would come.

All through the three months people were praying—not just missionaries in this big mid-India railway city, or those of our mission—but Anglo-Indians were praying. The Church of England services made room in their ritual for special prayer for Everett's recovery. The Catholics prayed. Back at the mission our Indian people who had received us with reservation were now praying night and day. Little children prayed for the recovery of the sahib with the bedtime prayer and finally, as things worsened, at every mealtime. It was no longer a personal matter for me and my children. The whole area prayed for a miracle. Differences were forgotten. The wait-and-see attitude of Christian workers who viewed us with some indifference were now one with us in loving concern, and their faith often helped mine.

In May he finally turned a corner and showed clear signs of recovery, but the heat was so intense that he could not cope with it, nor could his heart stand the mountain resorts of the Himalayan foothills, so we were sent to Australia, where we were suddenly dropped into midwinter.

Plans to go were made hastily and by cable with the Mission Board at home. They gave their permission and cabled the money. The red tape was cut away eventually, and in a matter of days we were off to Bombay with all papers and travelers' checks made out in my name in case my husband did not make it.

There was no time to go up to the mountains to see David. It was a matter of life and death to get Everett out of India and the scorching heat as soon as possible, so I wrote David and told him that we were taking our vacation in Australia because his father was weak and needed to get into a cold climate. David was already in boarding school, and I hoped he would understand that since we had to be separated anyway, it would not make so much difference whether we were on the plains of India or Australia since we would be coming to him on our return.

There was no choice about leaving David; he had to be in school. There was no money to take him, and Everett needed all the time and care I could give, but the trauma was greater on the lad of seven than I ever imagined.

How is it that at times in our lives the decision to save one loved one becomes the undoing of another? There is no doubt that David suffered acutely and that this insecurity produced in him fears and hostilities that made a profound change in his happy, trustful nature.

He was old enough to know we had left India, that we had left without him, and that his father might not be able to return. He knew his security was gone and that he alone of our family was left behind in India.

There are always those to comfort mothers who say that he will be fine, he won't know the difference, to remind one that there is really no choice, that he is far better off in school with other children. But David was far too sensitive, too aware, and too frightened. He worried more than anyone realized; his letters were brave, stereotyped. But I thought I could sense his understanding and acceptance, and so we took four-year-old Barbara, who was recovering from an illness, and we went by train to Bombay. We took the P & O SS *Strathmore* bound for Brisbane, touching Perth, Melbourne, Adelaide, and Sydney on the way.

We had no idea where we would settle. Not knowing anyone, we had no guide, but we decided we would go to the end of the line at Brisbane and make up our minds on the way back. The sea voyage was doing Everett a great deal of good.

Finally, on the return trip, we settled on Sydney. It was Friday evening when we disembarked, and we took a taxi—but where? All the hotels were filled. National sports events were on, and nowhere could we find a room. The city was swarming with people. We tried the YWCA, and they were willing to take Barbara and me, but Everett had to go to the YM down the street a distance.

It was very cold, the bed was cold, and Everett's circulation was poor. He had no hot water, so I filled the hot water bottle in the YW and hid it under my coat, walking down the street and up the stairs to Everett's room to get him through the night, taking Barbara back with me.

The situation was impossible. Everett was far too weak to be left. We had to find something.

Saturday morning we went to the P & O office to collect mail and make plans for our return in two months. There were letters—one from the family in America saying they felt it a great mistake for us to go to Australia instead of returning home. It was depressing to feel we were possibly out of God's will, and I prayed for some sign that God would let us know He was with us in this big city. Just then, as we were standing at the counter talking to the ship's agent, the telephone rang. The voice said, "There are passengers on the *Strathmore* by the name of Cattell. We want to get in touch with them. Can you help us?"

"They are standing right here!" was the reply, and the phone was given to me.

Total strangers, but relatives of the family who had helped me with Barbara on shipboard, called to say they wished to have us for dinner after church on Sunday. They asked to meet us at the Baptist church where they attended. They were so cordial, so warm, so very comforting! It was our sign. God was in Australia . . . in Sydney . . . with us, and we took heart.

Sunday morning we found our place in church; the usual hymn singing was over and the collection taken. Suddenly the words of the Scripture got our attention. What was this we were hearing? It was as though we had never heard the words before; the minister was reading 2 Corinthians 1:8-11:

> For we would not, brethren, have you ignorant of our trouble which came to us in Asia, that we were pressed out of measure, above strength, insomuch that we despaired even of life: but we had the sentence of death in ourselves, that we should not trust in ourselves, but in God which raiseth the dead: who delivered us from so great a death, and doth deliver: in whom we trust that he will yet deliver us; ye also helping together by prayer for us, that for the gift bestowed upon us by the means of many persons thanks may be given by many on our behalf.

Could the minister have chosen more suitable Scripture? It was unbelievable, and the words rang in my ears, "He will *yet* deliver us!"

Our hosts found us and took us to their home. The house was cold. No one noticed but us, but we had not then learned what we came to know: fires are luxuries to be had at teatime, not before! The Australian housewife seldom broke this rule. The food was delicious, and the hospitality most gracious, and hearing of our two nights in separate Y's, the newly found friends kept us with them until they could find a place for us to go out in the bush and orange grove community of Kurrajong.

We met with kindness everywhere. Everett was getting stronger, and finally the weeks passed, and it was time to return to India. He had written a book, and I had knit sweaters, a coat dress for Barbara, and sweaters for the boys of the family—but the main business was accomplished: Everett was a well man, and we were going back to India—and especially to David.

Had we gone to America, the Indians would have felt deserted and their prayers lost. There might have been a question of our return. Leaving David there was proof that we were serious about returning to India, but we did not know then the suffering David experienced. The cost to him was very great.

We had been gone from the mission nine months, but when we returned we were received with open arms, and everybody had had their own private answer to prayer. Everett's presence was the answer to every child and every adult. Even the Hindus had prayed, and some had promised to believe in the Christians' God if the sahib got well and returned.

How much is accomplished by uninterrupted work? How much by sacrifice? How much by suffering? How much by helplessness? How much by death—or life restored?

No man can tell. In God's hand, things are not what they seem, and victory rises from seeming defeat, and there is a healing in sickness nigh unto death that cannot come any other way. And where God is, and where faith is, miracles are not far away.

Our third year we won the hearts of our people, not by our preaching or by our outstanding work. It was not by any work at all, only by suffering and helplessness and letting them pray us through. This, too, is "missionary work," a method that none of us would ever choose, but its fruits were precious because, perhaps, of its cost not only to us but to all those who went with us through the ordeal, particularly to our son who was left in India to attend school while we were seeking health for his father.

The fellowship we sought in service together was found in our absence, and the three years that followed were years of concentrated efforts at evangelism—in the church, in the village, through the church and prolonged visits in villages that had been barely visited. All kinds of experiments were made until now, at the end of our first term, we were eager for furlough.

Chapter 4

Perspective

WE HAD BEEN IN INDIA six and a half years. It was the full term and time for furlough, and the word was spelled with capital letters! David carried America in his heart constantly, and in his memory as well. Every room of the parsonage we had left behind was etched upon his five-year-old memory; and as he grew older and bigger in size, so also did his memories of his native land as well as his dreams of what it would be like now, until the two were mingled together in one grand Utopia that to him was his America. He often said, "My America."

Barbara being only ten months old upon arrival in India had no memory of America at all, but David had shared his dreams with her.

The excitement grew with new dimensions of her vision of America until she, too, was aflutter with anticipated wonder.

As for my husband and me, our first term had been an unglorious and frustrating experience.

There were exciting victories in the village with some real hope of converts, only to have it canceled out by some crisis in the church when some trusted elder or leader would fall into sin and the news of it spread faster than wildfire and enormous loss of faith and shame resulted.

We were frankly discouraged, and I really wanted to get away for a complete change.

Shortly before we were due to leave, Everett came to me one day with the news that no one had been found to come out and take our place. The war was still on. We were too short-handed to leave without some extra help. It was difficult to find passage coming or going.

"Wouldn't it just be much better for us to stay for the duration? Actually, the board has suggested this with the offer of six months of vacation in South India."

The subject was not really open for debate. We would remain in India, but for how long? No time limit? Maybe years?

A deep depression took hold of me. My older brother Charles was even then in concentration camp near Shanghai, China. His wife had gotten to America safely. My younger brother Ezra, the surgeon, had also been in China at the time of the Japanese attack, but it had been possible for him to get to America after two years separation from his wife and daughters. At the time I did not know this and had no knowledge about either of my brothers. I felt desperately the need to talk to someone—to pray with someone—to have the fellowship of some woman who would reach out to me and understand.

I walked restlessly back and forth, thinking of the children, their disappointment, our own discouragement. Everywhere I looked—out toward the villages—up toward the hospital—to the church close by—darkness and despair seemed to hang over them all like a heavy cloud. This is India. Everyone said it would be hard here, but we had been so hopeful, so sure of the *promises*, so enthusiastic, and so full of plans that surely should have led to success—and now we were trapped here. If only I had some of my own people. If only I could get help so as not to add to the burdens Everett must feel, too!

I walked out to the back of the house to where the Indian families lived. The evangelist's wife, Ramki Bai, was sitting on the ground grinding her spices on a flat stone, rolling a rounded stone over the onions, tomatoes, and herbs, which results in a curry paste. She looked so absorbed and content and solid and wholesome, doing the work women have been doing for centuries, quickly with great vigor. Soon I was sitting on the corner of the rope bed talking to her, drawn by the peace that enveloped her.

"Ramki Bai," I began, "I need a sister or a friend today to talk to." I told her about my brothers having been caught in the war in China. I told her we could not go home now, with no idea when we could go.

"You know," I said, "What I need is *people* of my own, and the thought has come to me that you are my sister and friend. This is what Christian fellowship really is, isn't it? Why cannot my Indian Christian friends be my people? God gave us to each other—not just that we work here for India, but that you and I work together and help each other."

On and on we talked—happiness was flitting about within reach once more. Such sympathy flowed out from this little woman. She knew suffering. She knew sorrow, tragedy. How could one find a better friend?

I came back into the house refreshed. We had prayed together, and never shall I forget how she prayed for my brothers. Never in the world then did I dream that one day my younger brother, the surgeon, would bring his family to India—to our very town, our hospital—and share with us the joys and burdens of that work. Nor did she dream she would ever see him!

Since that time the Indian Christians became my people in a very real way. We began to do things together. I took them with me on trips to the villages. We visited in homes of villagers together, the patients in hospitals, in preaching camps, and in each other's homes. The women were organized. It was three and a half years before furlough time really came, but these years were the priceless ones; and it was in this time that our spiritual sons were born into the kingdom and we began to see fruit.

As thoughts of America faded, the war came closer to India. The British regiments swarmed our countryside. The jungles of our area were used for practice for jungle warfare in Burma. Jeeps and trucks passed constantly on the road in front of our house.

David set up a tea shop at the gate with an enormous tin teakettle boiling on a little charcoal burner on the ground. He borrowed a long unused table and set out his cups and saucers, which he borrowed from me. He hired the services of our cook, who baked cakes for him after his work was done in the bungalow. Those who saw the industry of this fourteen-year-old lad shared their sugar ration, as it was very limited for everyone. The British soldiers passing by, seeing an American lad at a tea stall, stopped, chatted, had a homemade cake and tea from a porcelain cup. Some of them were Christian lads. All of them were homesick, and David's time was occupied.

At the end of the winter vacation, he had a collection of army insignias, and after all bills were paid, enough rupees to pay his fare to South India for the Maramon Convention, where 40,000 Christians gathered for ten days in what was then Travancore and where his father was the preacher.

Being the only boy in the missionary family during the entire nine years, except for a little lad of three—the son of a lady doctor—he made friends with Indian boys.

The Christian lads of his age went hunting with him, and they brought back meat for Christmas dinner for the entire Christian community. He kept us in meat at a time when food of any kind was difficult. There were no parcels from home in that entire time, and everyone struggled for food.

I took pillow cases to Jhansi, hoping to fill them with flour and sugar, but rations did not extend to those out of the city, so in the end we learned to make our own flour. A woman living nearby ground the grain and brought in little piles of cracked wheat for cereal, graham flour which we used for everything except cake. For that we sifted the whole wheat flour through muslin. It was slow, but satisfactory. It was—in fact—all there was. Bread made from such flour does not keep from one day to the next, and we were *really* living in India. The war threatened, and soldiers were everywhere, Indian, British, and out beyond us—in the big cities—Americans.

We were most grateful for the meat the men brought to us, as the local fish, chickens, and eggs were being used by the army. David was a good shot. He was very careful with the use of his gun, and soon farmers came in from the village asking him to help protect their crops from wild boar and other wild animals that threatened their fields. Many were the nights he sat out in their fields—watching while he let the tired farmer doze. He became a friend to the villagers. The Maharajah heard of this and invited David to a big tiger hunt. They also became friends.

One day a village Christian said to me, "We have chosen David Sahib for our missionary. When he comes back from America, we will build him a house and he will live with us and teach us. He is one of us."

I thought then of what a terrific advantage he had. He did not have to win their love and confidence as we had done, nor struggle for the language as we still had to do. He spoke as one of them. He had adjusted perfectly to India. But I was concerned that these nine and a half years would unfit him for life in America, and my fears were not unfounded.

Chapter 5

Flowers and Buds

WE WERE IN INDIA nine and a half years before it was possible for us to leave the country. The war was still on, but we got passage on the rescue ship *Gripsholm* along with refugees from China and Greece. Steaming into the New York Harbor, we saw the Statue of Liberty. The passengers stood on the deck weeping with joy and pride, and we were among them.

The year of furlough was spent largely on the farm at Sunnyslope where Ezra and Frances and three children lived. Ezra was now the doctor of the rural community and a surgeon with fellowship in the American College of Surgeons.

It was also the year when Mary Catherine was born. David was now fifteen and Barbara eleven, when along came the beautiful baby girl named after her grandmother Mary Isabella and great-grandmother Mary and my sister, Mary Elizabeth, who had died in China so many years before.

Charles was also at home, having just escaped again from China and concentration camp in Shanghai. I had not seen him for fourteen years. There were times when their two girls, Margaret and Esther, with Ezra's three children (the twins, Pris and Pat, and little two-year-old Joe), and our three were at the farm at the same time.

What a happy year it was when the three of us were together with our families!

The year passed very quickly, and we took our three back to India on the Motor Ship *Adder*—sailing from San Francisco

—an Army transport ship so recently changed over to accommodate passengers that the paint was still wet when we went aboard.

We sailed out of the harbor into a full storm at sea. Christmas Day was a total flop, as no one was able to enjoy the day. Some were too seasick. The food fell off the tables, the chairs crashed into each other as the ship rocked and pitched, and the crew was too busy keeping the ship afloat.

Mary Catherine was four months old. She promptly got both ship dysentery and pneumonia. There were twenty-four women and children crowded in together in our double-decker stateroom.

Early one morning the engine stopped; the electricity went off. It was dark and we were at the mercy of the waves. All the things stored under the bunks started to roll, banging against the wall opposite and then started back as the ship shook itself out of one trough into another, when everything came tumbling back against the other side. There were suitcases, apples, tinned food for children, baby bottles, potties, toys, shoes, whatever was loose. It was all mingled together as the ship turned on one side and then another, banging and rolling and generally mixed.

It was soon apparent that we were in real danger. The electricity being off, there was no light, no loud speaker, no way to give orders. Mothers with babes in arms sat on the edge of their bunks and packed handbags with survival necessities in case we had to go to lifeboats. One woman had an accordion that she managed to open and to play softly, "Master, the Tempest Is Raging." We moved closer together near the music, and we sang all the hymns we knew that mentioned storms at sea: "Rock of Ages" and many others came to mind as we sang and prayed for the quieting of the storm.

Our menfolk were in another room, and we had no instructions whatever while we rocked and pitched in the tempest.

After a while the lights came on and also the hum of the motor in the engine room. We were now under control again, and we mothers crawled back to our bunks to await the day. The storm raged on, but we were able to move out of it in a few days, but not until after three fourths of the ship's dishes were broken by falling off the tables. There were seventeen passengers with broken bones. We had lost a lifeboat, and there was general disorder and trouble everywhere, but we did arrive in India, and the children had a happy winter before they started back to boarding school in March.

The Indians were delighted to have us bring a baby back with us. The women slipped up to me during our welcome program and said, "You know we prayed that you would bring a baby back with you."

"Oh, so that was what happened?" I responded. "Don't pray that any more. I am too old! But thank you for Mary Catherine. We are glad to have her."

Now when both children were back at Woodstock in school, we had a baby to give us cheer and keep us young. The first word Mary learned was Hallelujah! It is a good word in both languages!

Again we were faced with the problem of someone to care for the baby. By this time village work was wide open to me with responsibility for the women's evangelistic work of the mission. I could neither take the baby nor leave her. After a few false attempts, a man and his wife came to us to be cook and *ayah.* She had never worked before. She was not a "professional"—she was just a very warmhearted gentlewoman, a Christian, and a genuinely lovely person. Mary Catherine adored her, and I found then and through the years that I had to share Mary Catherine's love with Bai ji. She had self-respect and the respect of all who knew her, and I often wondered at the goodness of God in finding her for me. There was no need for anxiety when Bai ji was in the house. After her husband died, she found comfort and dignity in her work with us, and we all found comfort in her presence.

The year after our return to India, my brother Ezra, the doctor-surgeon, and Frances, his wife, and their four children started out to return to China. All trunks, boxes, and drums were packed and sent to the West Coast, where they also waited for weeks for passage to Shanghai. However, word came through that Nanking had fallen to the Communists and all hope of going back to China was gone.

What were they to do? The doctor's practice was sold; the way ahead as well as behind was closed. As they prayed and waited for further direction from the Lord, it became clear that they should go to India and join our mission staff there, taking over the medical work.

Who ever could imagine such a thing that two of us should be assigned to the same station—Ezra and I with our families!

Everett and I went to Bombay to meet them and had the joy of introducing them to Bombay, to the train ride up country, to the mission, and Indian life.

The women's hospital became a general hospital. It was enlarged, and the patients came from all over the area. Missionaries came from other parts of India for needed surgery.

Once when Ezra was down with hepatitis and very ill, a nurse came with the word that a woman was in labor and an emergency had developed that could cost her life and the life of the baby. I saw Ezra carried on a stretcher to the operating room, where he operated and saved the lives of mother and child while nearly losing his own. The memory of that incident will stay with me always as an example of the truth that to save others one cannot always save themselves!

As other missionaries came to join us, we included them in our family circle. At one time there were fifteen missionaries on the field, and fourteen children. Those were wonderful days of advancement in the work of the mission, as well as for the missionary fellowship.

During council meetings, which often lasted over three days, Barbara and David would organize fun for the children.

In March there was a general exodus when all the missionary children six years old or over started off with tin trunks and bedding rolls for the mountains, where for nine months they would be in school.

Did parents ever get used to this separation? No, we never did, though it was an every-year experience. Neither did the children. It was just one of the things that had to be. In the case of small children under six, the separation was not long, as by April or May it was too hot on the plains, and mothers took them off to the cool of the Himalayan foothills and joined the children who had gone ahead.

Chapter 6

In the Shadow of Eternal Snows

India was to me divided into only two parts: the hills and the plains. And while the distance between was roughly only 500 miles, in a land of slow travel and poor communication, it was a distance great enough to tear many a mother's heart in two!

In these twenty years how many times I had gone to the mountains for the hottest months, and in all manner of ways, seldom able to sit on a train like a lady in comfort! Sometimes I was lying on the luggage rack, or climbing out of the train windows when there were too many tin boxes pushed against the compartment door. Or I waited for hours for a belated train, lying on the bedding roll on the floor of a waiting room . . . or even resting on a table under the great *punkahs*, or fans. Thus I kept reasonably comfortable, though the heat of Indian trains in Indian hot season is most unreasonable.

Travel in India was always exciting. The Indian scene, while passing by on the moving train or observing people crowded around any railway station, is a drama of unparalleled fascination.

It was shortly before the British withdrew from India. There was a general unrest and anti-British propaganda. The trains were crowded with soldiers, and pilgrims and travel was rough and uncertain. It was October and I had not seen the children in boarding up in the hills since the first of July. Word came that they needed me, and so I took the first train I could get to Delhi, arriving with ten minutes to spare to catch the

Punjab Mail, which would take me to Saharanpur with an eighty-mile bus ride at daybreak from there to Landour to the hill station where the children were.

As it happened, there was an antiforeign demonstration on the Delhi station platform when my train pulled in. It was nearing time for election, and the Congress Party was proving to the crowds that they were no stooges of the British, nor of any white people. They agreed that no white person would get on a train that night.

Totally unaware, I ran after the coolie who had my suitcase and bedding roll balanced on his head making way for me to get through the jostling crowds before the next train pulled out. The green flag was waving and the guard was blowing his whistle, ready to go, when breathlessly, I said, "Please, sir, I must get on this train. Can you help me, sir?" I implored of the Anglo-Indian guard.

"I will see what I can do. Get in the ladies compartment. I cannot hold the train any longer."

There was no room and the women within refused to open the door. The guard and I then raced from compartment to compartment filled with Congress Party leaders.

"You cannot enter, madam," they said in polite but mocking English.

"I'll sit on my own luggage. I do not ask a seat—only that I may get in . . ." but "No, madam" was the answer all up and down the train, which was puffing and steaming impatient to be gone.

"Madam," said the guard, "just get in—don't ask. I'll open the door to the women's compartment. Get in and say nothing. There is trouble tonight on the platform. Once out of Delhi, you will be all right, but no matter what happens, say nothing."

I got in. The train started and my luggage came in through the window. I threw the money to the coolie and we were off. In a moment we came to a sudden and grinding halt. Each compartment jumped wildly into the one in front and then backed into the one behind—with a jolt. Someone had pulled the cord that automatically stopped the train. A crowd gathered outside my compartment. "Get her out," they cried. "No foreigner is going anywhere tonight." I sat still and looked the other way as though I had no idea who or what was the cause of the trouble. The guard came into the compartment and asked each of us women for our tickets. Men from the next compartment demanded that I be put off.

"Where is your ticket?" the guard asked of the women across from me. There was an old woman servant of a beautiful, very modern and charming woman and her old mother-in-law and a few small children smartly dressed.

"These are my women," replied the man who kept insisting that I get out.

"Let me see their tickets," the guard demanded.

"Well, you see. I have a ticket for myself. These women are in my party," replied the gentleman.

"Where is their ticket?"

"Well, Sir. You see, Sir; I saw no need to buy a ticket for these women."

The crowds outside came closer and finding the leading agitator caught in the embarrassing predicament without a ticket for his party, they backed away and laughed among themselves. The man and the guard then became the center of attention. He finally paid the fare for his womenfolk, got back in the men's compartment, and we were really off.

The women fell into a conversation then as women in India always do, and all was pleasantness again.

"How far are you going?" they asked me in English.

"To Saharanpur," I replied in Hindi. "How far are you going?" also in Hindi.

"To Saharanpur also. Oh! I see you understand and speak our langauge."

"Oh, yes—I have lived in India many years."

Now they were embarrassed as they knew I had understood the whole situation about not wanting me, and also that they had tried to get by without a ticket.

We started talking about our children—always a safe and comfortable subject for mothers.

"We have a son in Woodstock School in Landour," they admitted. "We have not seen him for several months and we think he is homesick and needs to have a visit."

"That is very interesting indeed," I replied (and all our conversation was easy now and in Hindi). "You know, I also have a son in Woodstock School and I am going to the hills for the very same reason."

As it turned out, our sons were classmates and the best of friends.

I pondered many things that night when my bitter opponents, now my friends, had gone to sleep. How is it that they would send their son to an American school and yet make a scene against one American woman? But I knew. There are times when politics demand a show of independence and hostility against those for whom we have the deepest respect. It happens everywhere.

The compartment was so crowded by the time we reached Saharanpur that I had to climb out the window. The grinning guard was there to catch me as I fell out on the platform. The women put my luggage out after me, and the gentleman who had been so eager to put me off the train was busy prying the compartment door open to get his women out properly. He spoke warmly and we went our way. Once the political pressure was off, we were just concerned parents homesick for our boys in boarding school—boys in the same class of the same school and the best of friends.

Cholera was abroad in the land, as is so often the case after the rains, so I ate no food, but hot tea, India's lifesaver, was bountiful and safe as well as reviving after a sleepless night, with excitement of many sorts thrown in free of charge.

A bus ride of eighty miles in the early morning was the last lap of the journey to the mountain. At a certain place in a mountain gap, the fresh breeze from off the snows reached us. It was unfailing and unmistakable. This was the mountain air—relief from the heat, the refreshment thousands of people in North India plains sought each summer. Mussoorie was not far away, and just beyond it, Landour—and the school and somewhere there—my children!

Soon the tin roofs of the hill station appeared and the shops and stores clinging to the steep mountainsides like barnacles to a ship. How the frail, flimsy houses in the narrow bazaar keep from falling down the mountain has always been a mystery—but year after year they cling to the wet, dark streets of Landour, their shops perched on either side, giving out the spicy pungent odor of food cooking in hot fat.

Tehri Road is the main road leading back to the mountain villages and towns. Charcoal came along on the backs of coolies in bags suspended with a band across the forehead or with help from a rope slung across both shoulders. Luggage came up the mountain on the backs of coolies—mounds of luggage. All who came to the hills had to have their belongings carried in this way. Donkey trains carried stoves, wood, sacks of potatoes, and merchandise to and fro, and people unable to climb ascended in sedan chairs with a floor in the bottom of the chair, unlike the sedan chairs of the China mountains. Four men carried the chair; for me it was the last lap of the long road to our children. (All this has been changed with a motor road in recent years.)

At first it seemed cruel to put such heavy burdens on human backs, but these men had come for the summer months from their villages, walking for many days for the express purpose of this privilege, to carry burdens and thus make their extra cash in a barter economy during the slack months of farming. Coolies fought over every suitcase, bedroll, or tinbox. Police kept them from hurting one another in the mad rush to get a load. Paying them off was always difficult. Enough was never enough. To give more upset the economy for all. What was just and right was a hard amount to determine except as a rate was fixed by the municipality, which in later years it was.

And now with the coolies paid and the hill house opened up by the *chaukidar* (caretaker), I quickly put the house in order and put up the pictures and the curtains. Through the years I had lived in thirteen of those houses on the hill. In our first nine years, we had no hill home, and we rented where we could. Some were very poor quarters by any standard. Once we lived in the coolie quarters, which were so blackened by smoke—for the coolies cooked right on the cement floor of the

The Cattell family go for a week in the jungle

Barbara and her ayah Kali Bai

Camping in Bundelkhand

David with Carrie Wood in ox cart

Alene Calkins with Barbara and Claude Fraser Bennett

Mary Catherine with her ayah
and Micky the dog

Mary Catherine
with Prince

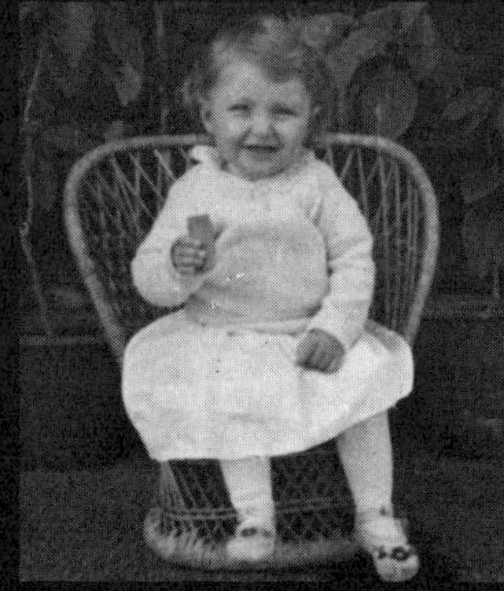

Barbara
Anne

Mary's ayah
(baby-sitter)

Chhatarpur home

Esther Baird (center), retiring pioneer missionary of Ohio Friends, receiving the gold Kaiser-i-Hind reward from the British Government Agency personnel — and David.

Sending the children off to boarding school

Woodstock school spread out over the mountain

Hiking in the mountains. Barbara in basket

In Australia. Everett, Catherine, and Barbara Ann

Father and daughter going places

Catherine and friends

Barbara and Indian village girl

The family at home in Chhatarpur

David and his python

High school girl in the mountains (Barbara)

David and his friend and a wild boar

Barbara, Mary Catherine, and David with pets, Chhatarpur

David and Jane's wedding

Arrested: Stuti Prakash, Pastor; Everett Cattell, Supt.; Samson Heiri Lal, M & O Chairman. After court trial was over–

rooms—it took eight coats of whitewash to get the walls even a light beige color; our furniture in the living room consisted of trunks put end to end along one whole side covered with comforts for padding. This was the davenport. We had one table and one chair and, lo, the living room was furnished!

Then we built one hill house and bought another for our growing mission family, and in the later years we enjoyed one of the nicer homes on the hill; but wherever our home, the pictures and curtains went up right away and a tablecloth on the table. Whatever kind of stove we had—charcoal, oil, or electric—was soon going—getting water hot for tea. Whatever flowers were about and in season were plucked and put in a vase; and when school was out, in bounded the children to home and to my arms! I never wanted them to come to a bleak house, so we did the homey things first and unpacked and settled in properly while they were at school the next day.

Such simple things make the poorest house homey, and to this day our children have no memory of starkness or barren rooms. Every house was home, and there are priceless and precious memories in each of the thirteen houses.

Barbara's hair was parted in a zigzag kind of way, and she looked shabby and forlorn as boarders often do. The personal and individual care was impossible, but as she grew older, she came home to me looking very chic and neat.

But David—one year he grew a whole foot, and in October, at the time when I felt he needed me, I was not mistaken. His pants were far too short, his shoes too small. He was walking on bare ground with holes in his shoes so large he could barely keep his shoes on his feet, and he looked as though he needed a mother.

There was no way to outfit him with ready-mades, but we called the *darzi* (tailor) and the *mochi* (cobbler), and once again self-respect and confidence were restored. The cost of missionary work is nowhere so painful as in the separation of children from parents, but because of this the time we had together was priceless.

On the plains of Central India we lived in an isolated world of our own with our own people in an area that was large enough considering it was the only mission among three-quarters of a million people—but only occasionally did we see other foreign missionaries.

On the hills of Landour, it was quite the other way; there were 500 other missionaries attending the same Union Church, sending children to the same school—and the new missionaries coming to North India studied Hindi at the language school that was held on weekdays at the Union Church.

There was a great deal of activity during these summer months when life straddled the India-America culture, but, as in Kuling, China, years ago, children attending the American school took on American ways. There were always some who had just returned from furlough who kept the others informed of the new teenage vocabulary and the new styles.

The new missionaries coming out were watched eagerly for the styles current in the homeland, and the length of our years in India could be fairly accurately judged by the clothes we wore.

Our children were living through the same double life-style that my brothers and I experienced in China—Orientals on the plains and something akin to American-hood in the mountains. However, my children had nine months of the school year in this semiwestern atmosphere, while with me and my brothers, it was just during vacation time in the summer. In India the school year was from March to November to escape the heat, and especially the steaming rains.

Chapter 7

Over the Rainbow

OUR CHILDREN REACTED very differently to boarding school. David suffered from the beginning and never learned to enjoy dormitory life, although he dearly loved the mountains. There were bullies among the older boys, and the younger ones were threatened with dire punishment if they told their parents, teachers, or anyone of their treatment from the older boys. David spent much of his free time alone to avoid them. It was years before we discovered the reason for his dread of school.

He loved nature, and his room at home was often a nursery for baby animals he found on the mountain. We lived for a few summer seasons at Hearthstone. It was our first comfortable home in the hills. There was a long living-dining room across the front of the house facing the valley below in view of the school. The kitchen, hall, and bedroom backed up to the mountain. Downstairs opened up on another terrace where there were three more rooms, a storeroom, bedroom, and workshop.

We had boarders living in the home with us, so every nook was filled. David had the workbench for his bed, under which he kept his wild pets. At one time it was a baby jackal, but he kept it a secret from me until after it died. At another time he had snakes in a drawer in his room. This also I did not know until later! At one time he even had me collecting snakes for his school project—but I saw to it that they were dead ones. I had collected for Charles as a girl and now for David. Our menfolk were great collectors of specimens of all kinds.

David was a brave lad. He feared nothing, and often when I cautioned him about his trip into the mountains or taking health precautions or the danger of snakes, he would reply in his wry way in Hindi, "*Ma, teri bishwas kahan hai*?" "Mother, where is your faith?"

David got behind a year due to furlough coming at the wrong time. I had had the same problem years before, but David did not have the understanding help I had to make up the year. It was the reason for his losing interest in school and his grades were a great concern to me, but when graduation time came, he passed, and his father and I went to the mountains in November for the occasion.

It was cold—bitter cold—at night. There was no heat in any of our homes or school except for a fireplace that warmed only slightly what was directly in front of it. The rains were over and the sky clear without a cloud. The snows were out with their white peaks piercing the deep blue of the sky. The air was clear. We could see the plains below us and the Himalayas above us with seven blue and purple ranges between. It was a glorious time for our little family as we lived those last happy days together before David left Landour for America.

Everett preached the baccalaureate sermon for David's class. The song the parents composed for the class was put to the tune of "Over the Rainbow," and I never hear its haunting tune now without feeling once more the poignancy of that night when we parents sang to our sons and daughters in Landour of the Himalayan foothills.

David spent his last Christmas on the plains with us, hunting for our Christmas meat, visiting the camping parties in the villages, going with me by bicycle to my outstation preaching missions. We stayed in homes of Indian Christians, David sleeping with the menfolk of the family and I with the women, children, and crying babies, along with rats that rattled around among the pots and pans looking for a morsel of food. We cycled long distances together, he in front making a path for me between rocks and skirting the thorn trees and through river beds.

One night in the village of Gulganj the family was having a celebration with the three Christian families living there. It was my birthday. We had a battery radio with us. After a chicken curry and rice dinner, sitting on the floor of the old *dak* bungalow that the British had at one time used for a rest house, we fell into conversation about India and the conditions of unrest; David turned the radio on just as Nehru, the prime minister, spoke those immortal words: "The Light of India has gone out. Mr. Gandhi is dead, killed by an assassin."

It would have been long before the word would have come to this remote village, but our radio brought it to them instantly. For the first time in history, the little village was up to date on world news.

David and I left the next morning for Bijawer, where I was to preach Sunday, staying overnight with an Indian family. The wife was one of our orphan girls and the husband one of David's dearest friends. We brought the bad news of Gandhi's assassination to that State capital, and the good news of Jesus Christ, our living Savior, to those who would hear. David was a great help to me, as I would never have dared the long bicycle trips alone. There were many dangers, and I was helpless with flat tires and finding my way over unmarked cowpaths.

All too soon David's time to sail for America and college arrived. It would be three years before we could hope to see him again. Ezra, my surgeon brother now in India, and my husband went together to Bombay to see David off. David went alone as far as companions were concerned. The sight of David standing by himself on the deck waving to his father, his uncle, and the whole familiar life of India, even India itself, was one of the saddest experiences my husband has ever had. It was heartrending for all of us. David dreaded it so terribly. He loved India and the Indians loved him. Would God bring him back some day? I hoped in my heart He would.

David spent a few days in England with the soldier boys who had drunk tea at his tea stand during the war, which brought thousands of British soldiers to Bundelkhand for jungle war practice. A few were Christian lads, married now, who invited David to visit them.

America, his America, seemed very cold and impersonal to him. It was not the America he remembered. His reaction was entirely negative except for a boyhood sweetheart and her family. When that bright prospect turned to ashes he became aloof, and the years that followed were bleak indeed.

He resented the affluence of Americans in general. He had never had a room of his own in India. He either slept on the verandah or in the workshop or on a cot in the dining room or somewhere. We had only two bedrooms in our Indian home, and the girls used the other one, except when we had guests and we all took to verandahs or slept dormitory style. It bothered him that Americans had so much and shared so little.

The letters that came to us from shocked friends and concerned relatives were a heartbreak. What could we do out there so far away? David and our dear ones at home were not communicating, and for three years it looked like he was a lost boy. He was the first of our India missionary children to graduate in India and return for college, and the shock was traumatic for him, for those who knew him, and to us when various descriptions of his behavior reached us.

We were in the hills again when the letter came saying that David was hopeless and had been given up by our closest friends.

It was pouring rain. There was a prayer meeting of our mission family a few houses on down the mountain. We prayed for David, but my heart was not at rest. On the way back up with water rushing down past me as I climbed and rain beating against my face, my tears flowed mingled with the pelting rain, and I cried aloud to God.

How did this happen? How did he get so mixed up? What should we have done differently? There were no answers. In any case it was too late, and then a verse came out of the depths: "I *know* WHOM I have believed and am *persuaded* that HE IS ABLE to keep David." I knew that the verse said ". . . keep that which I have committed unto him," but to me that meant David and at that moment I committed him. It was a real experience, and a quiet peace stole over my spirit and I *knew* God was not giving David up though others had.

I also knew that I had not given him up but that I had given him to God.

Although we did not know it until much later, David went to church the next Sunday night and went forward to begin a long road back to God.

When we came back to America for furlough three years after he left India, he came to meet us with Everett's sister and family in New York. He had been through three agonizing years; though he was on the way back there was much to heal, and we were glad to have him home with us again. However there, too, he had to sleep in the kitchen on a folding cot. He never complained, too happy to be under the same roof once more.

One night while we were talking things over, past, present, and future, I said to David, "We have given you a rough time, Son, leaving you so many times, letting you suffer through those tender years in boarding, letting you come home alone. To us, we were following what we felt was God's call. You just had to come along with us and take the hard things." I was going to say that perhaps we would have been better advised to do more with reference to our children's best interests, but David would hear none of it.

"No, Mom, I've been proud of you and Dad for being real missionaries. I was proud you took God's call seriously and were willing to rough it. I'm glad, too, that you trusted me to understand. I did, and it made me feel a part of the whole team to take the hard with the good. It has been good!"

Home life was wonderful for him, and in my heart I *knew* God had not forgotten His promise.

David had been a part-time policeman, a resort "life saver." He had been a conscientious objector during the war, and his alternate service took him to Cleveland hospitals, where he was an orderly. His college work had suffered, but he was willing to go back and try again.

He had an old Ford coupe called "Monoxide Molly," which he drove off to college the week before we returned to India after a year of furlough. His Indian black buck horns were strapped to the front of his unmuffled car as he waved, "Goodbye," this time to make good and follow God.

I saved my tears until he was out of sight, and that was the last time we ever saw our son, but God *was* true and He *was* able and He *did* restore David to be a ministerial student set to return with his wife and child to India as missionaries, but they went to heaven instead.

Chapter 8

Hills and Plains

BARBARA WAS FOUR YEARS OLD when she went to what was known in the American School in the hill station as Lower Kindergarten and seemed to be flourishing among the little playmates she found there. On the plains she was not only alone with no missionary children to play with, but the Indian children were in school during the rains of July and August, so I accepted the invitation of a dear friend who lived with her children in the apartment below us in the hills. She had a little girl the same age, and she took Barbara in to give her a little longer in the healthful climate and among playmates.

There were missionary mothers among us who stayed with their children in the hills the entire nine months of school. The husbands and fathers came and went, but the children were provided with a home the year around. These women were missionary wives with no special assignment.

There were other mothers who were missionaries with responsibilities and salaries equal with the men of the mission; they had a very short time in which to visit their children who were in boarding most of the year. There were other women who, with or without assignment, felt it their duty to be with their husbands, feeling the children were well cared for in school. And there were those who were permitted to come and go as the needs required.

There were mothers who, making a home for their own children for a longer period, took in other children to give them a little home life.

We were among the stricter of missions regarding women, especially when our children were little. Six weeks for the men and two months for the women was the rule, so I counted on seven months of separation each year, which were the hardest part of my missionary life. It was always a comfort when another mother offered to take my children, and Barbara had her share of "other mothers"—one especially.

By the time Barbara was six, she too went into boarding. Rules were hard on little girls—the going-to-bed rules without loving care or stories or a hug, but along with the other children she learned not to cry and not to admit to homesickness. It was understood among the littlest ones even that this was just not done. So the hurts went untended and the little aches unsoothed. They developed a certain independence, and they reacted in their own ways to life in the dorm.

Barbara was a social little soul and had her friends at the house frequently when I was there. We had parties for her. There were boy friends galore with whom she was temporarily madly in love. She won the running races just as I had years ago in China.

Clothes were a great problem. We could not buy them in India, and the children so quickly grew out of the ones we took out from America. Mothers solved the problem by sponsoring a sale each season when all outgrown clothing was priced and put on display and bought by other mothers for children who needed that particular size. It was a great help, and the Indian tailors were able to make clothes from just pictures—no patterns; so we managed. Coats were difficult to come by. One year I had a red wool bathrobe made into a coat for Barbara, and we even put on a fur collar that came out of a missionary barrel. The Barter Sale became quite an institution in Landour. When mothers were through exchanging clothes to fit their growing children, the sale was opened to the public and became a much anticipated affair to all—servants and hill people alike.

BARTER SALE '57

I'm getting ready for the Barter Sale
With a tremendous amount yet to do,
To gather my rags
And sew on the tags
And hunt up that other good shoe.

To settle on prices—ah, that's the worst.
Will it sell for eight annas or not
When it's worth far more—
A dress I adore—
Though I've had it—how long—I've forgot!

The belts and hats and dishes and pans
Will look like junk at the sale.
And as people pass by
With a critical eye
Will check the minutest detail.

The things I can't wear will go cheap as can be
And the things that I like will go high.
No matter how much
It really is worth
Or its value to the keen passerby.

"My goodness, what a bargain I've found."
Or "What a price to ask for that dress!
There's a tear in the seam—
The style, a bad dream—
And the trimming is really a mess!"

Well, I think I'll send them along anyway
Though it seems a rather hard thing to do;
Take over the case—
Bringing my junk to disgrace,
But I'm out for real bargaining too!

What a shock yet to come, with the box back at home,
The suit and the dress did not go!
Even the coolie and cook

Had all had a look
And passed up what I marked so low!

So, let out the hem and wear them again.
I'm pleased those things did not sell.
I'll fix them like new,
Yes, that's what I'll do.
In fact, they look rather well!

Of course, next year—come Barter Sale
I'll send them in again without fail.
Marked low
They'll go!

As Barbara grew older, she developed a mind of her own about styles, and just not any old hand-me-down was so gratefully received; but she wore simple things well and looked nice, but was more and more aware of what everybody else was wearing. Since I was conservative myself, some of my ideas about clothes, social life, and conduct seemed less important to her than what her friends were doing.

In her high school years especially, she was active in speaking contests, singing groups, in the sextette, and all that went with school life.

One mother said to me, "The party always comes to life when Barbara comes into the room."

Barbara graduated in June. We had stayed in India eight years that term so that we could let her finish with her class instead of taking furlough at the usual time. We traveled home through Europe, bringing in our party three others of her classmates and Mary Catherine and an English lady doctor.

There were other parties going through Europe from the same class, and there were thirty of the seniors on the S.S. *Victoria* from Bombay to Naples. The members of the chorus and sextette were all on the ship. On Sunday when my husband was asked by the ship's captain to take the Sunday service, he had the Woodstock students sing the introit; the sextette sang the special and then the "Amen."

After ten marvelous days in Europe and three weeks in England we still had enough Woodstock seniors on the Motor

Ship *United States* to carry the music through the Sunday service, when my husband was again chosen to take charge. Even the sextette was still all together.

However, it was in England, at Keswick, during the week of conference when we were there as guests that Barbara went for a walk along a cold babbling stream with a missionary. Something happened that day, for when Barbara returned she was a changed girl. Her commitment to Christ had made the difference, and our fears for her in America were unwarranted. While in our church Bible college, she fell in love with a fine tall young preacher, John Brantingham, became his wife, and later a missionary, and is now the mother of four of the third generation of missionary children.

Mary's childhood was completely different from that of our other two. By the time she came along, there were six little girls in the mission and about the same age. She had playmates, both Indian and American. About that time we had dogs—dachshunds the British left behind when they so abruptly turned India over to the Indians and returned to England. The dogs begat dogs, and the little girls and the two little boys of the mission had black miniature puppies running at their heels. It was difficult to find Indian homes for them because of the extra expense involved in feeding and caring for dogs of special breeding. Mongrels have heartier appetites and can exist while dachshunds have to be fed!

Mary organized the children on the compound. There were Mohammedan, Hindu, and Christian; but when Mary rang the bell, they all came running to play. When we came home in the evening from the village, she ran to meet us with her arms outstretched, eager to tell us all the details of the day's activities, which were to her important matters. After she finished telling us her news she would sit quietly for a moment and then, in a businesslike way, look up and say, "Now tell me your 'bats' (affairs)."

One day Bai ji said to me, "Memsahiba, Mary seems to be able to manage the mission all by herself." I knew then that she had been bossing the servants as well as children and probably the mission workers as well, but I also knew that Mary *was* an organizer, and I recognized both the gift and problems with which she would have to deal. She did a lot of advising even as a little girl, as her friends discussed their problems with her.

As a result of a fall down the mountain at the age of four, she developed very severe back trouble. As she grew older it became so serious that she had to be hospitalized and then put in a brace for a year. She was very tall for her age, and I feared for her schooling inasmuch as we had already had to make up one year's work to compensate for furlough. I taught her again during the summer, but as the time came for me to go to the plains and back to work it became apparent that she could neither go with me on the long journey by train nor enter boarding school, so I had to stay up in the hill house with her and look after her until well into November.

It was a long time to be away from my work, but my husband suggested that I write down the lessons that had emerged from the years of trying to communicate Christ and His teachings to the illiterate and backward people of our area. Sitting in a dentist's office one day, I told a friend from a neighboring mission about my predicament. As it turned out, she was an artist and longed to do just the kind of artwork I needed in order to illustrate my lessons. Her mission loaned her to work with me and she came to live with us. Because she was a nurse, she was a great comfort and help; I was grateful for her companionship and her artistic talent.

In November the book was finished, and the same day Mary went back to boarding. It was very clearly God leading. He had helped and provided for all those difficult months. One day Mary said, "Mother, did I have to have this trouble so that you could write the book?"

"No," I replied, "God helped me to write the book because you needed me with you."

The name of the book was *That They May Know,* with ten lessons for non-Christians and ten for new Christians. These were translated in other languages of India and quickly spread over the entire subcontinent. It became my parting gift to India although I had no idea that we would be leaving when I wrote it.

Mary Catherine appeared to be the healthiest and most delightful of children, but health problems have continued to assail her, and she suffered in many ways and had some serious afflictions that made it necessary for her to be at home more than the other children were. She became quite a companion to me in times when she required my care and attention.

During the long summer while she was flat on her back, I heard of a litter of German police dogs whose mother had died, leaving them without much chance to live. The mother dog belonged at one time to a British officer who, in his hurry to leave India in 1957, left his Alsatian to his sweeper, who had the care of the dog. The servant now was frantic, losing his chance to sell the puppies, and offered them very cheaply to anyone who would take a pup.

I went over to see the unfortunate little orphans and brought one home to Mary Catherine. We nursed it to health, named him Prince, and at the end of the summer gave him to my husband, who didn't have much patience with little "under-foot" dogs and had longed for a big, well-bred dog of some intelligence and—well, Prince was the perfect answer. He turned out to be really a prince of a dog and he made all of us happy. Mary loved all her pets, but Prince was the pride of the whole family.

One year when she was very small, I took a trip with Mary, her baby buggy, two dogs on a leash, a cat in a basket, and two birds in a cage in addition to bedding rolls, suitcase, tin trunks, and water jars. There is so much hilarity in India. The most ridiculous situations ease difficult times. Laughter is very close by to sorrow! And sorrow softens harsh laughter. I have to laugh again at the mayhem of traveling with the "zoo"—dogs dashing in different directions, tangling chains around other passengers' legs, the cat almost getting out of the basket while I was trying to get all safely into an already crowded train, and the baby crying to boot!

Thank God for a sense of humor! And thank God for a memory that brings the funny things to mind when one is carrying a heavy heart. How beautifully balanced is life in the will of God!

Chapter 9
Birds in the Garden

OCTOBER IN MID-INDIA SEEMS TO KNOW just when to turn off the humid sultry heat of the monsoons and invigorate the drowsy atmosphere with a healing, drying quality that brings back the energy and the zest to work toward erstwhile soggy visions. This sudden change in the weather had been fixed for centuries at the fifteenth of the month and seldom has failed to keep to schedule.

One suddenly feels refreshed and eager to take hold of life. It is the time to plant flowers and vegetables, and it is the time to houseclean and whitewash inside and out. Indeed the whole of October is celebrated in Hindu communities with *Dhasera* and *Diwali* holidays, while the Christians use the month for conferences, conventions, and committees. India takes on new life in October. And everybody works at cleaning up the ravages of the rains.

For one thing, the gods are brought out again and given an airing and set up to deal with human affairs for the ensuing nine months, having had three months vacation in some dark paradise where the monsoons could not reach their sensitive exteriors and where there was no interference by the events and cries of suffering humanity during the rains. It is too much for the gods, and it is often too much for people who are heir to such afflictions as cholera and malaria and infections of all kinds that flourish in the humidity. It is the time when mud houses fall in and fires do not burn and funeral pyres do consume the dead; when wild animals prowl and snakes are washed out of their holes to jeopardize the lives of unsuspecting laborers. It is the time for ants to march and scorpions to bite, and the gods take cover in the underworld.

There is small wonder that the people of India celebrate so lavishly and so fanatically when the monsoons are over and the time has come again for rebuilding, redecorating, and rejoicing.

Never have I been so grateful for a year-round God as during the Indian monsoon, the One who cares about human need even during the rain and who sees His children through them.

It was just such a perfect day of drying out when a feeling of urgency took hold of me to get at the annual renovation within the house and in the garden.

The closets needed cleaning out, the clothes put out to dry, the mattresses put in the sun for hours, the storerooms emptied out and all the contents sunned, the mildewed books, shoes, and suitcases spread out, the white ants hunted down and their ravages salvaged or destroyed according to the extent of activity, the musty odors of trunks and bedding aired out, and finally the moving of all the furniture outdoors for the annual whitewash inside—room by room.

It was also time to get the *mali* at the garden. Winter gardens in India can be so beautiful, and now was the time to set the stage, plan the borders, and plant the beds.

I stood on the verandah of our brick house looking through its arched pillars toward the city a half mile away on the other side of the tombs that dotted the distance between. It was as though there was a grove of tombs planted there instead of trees. They were growing old and green with mold and moss, and little trees were emerging from the cracks and crevices that succeeding monsoons had driven deep within them.

As I watched the little path winding between them, I saw the *chaprassi* (messenger boy) coming toward me with the bag of mail, and I knew today there would be mail from America. For some reason I felt that there would be something special in it, something frightening perhaps, at least earthshaking to my small world. Already there was a disturbed, uneasy premonition within as I took the mail from the eager young man who handed it to me.

Letters from America did not come every day to the remote, out-of-the-way towns in Central India. When world affairs were not in a state of crisis, mail came fairly regularly, but it was always an event.

Kamla leaned the bicycle against the verandah and reached into the khaki mailbag for the letters. He handed the bundle of letters, the daily paper, and a magazine or two to me with a smile.

"Good foreign mail today, Memsahiba." He was always happy when there was lots of mail. It gave him a sense of importance when he stood at the post office with the other *chaprassis* from the city and watched the sorting to see the mission pile grow bigger than the others, and letters were so special that it was a good day when he had some to deliver here and there, and now it was my turn to get our share!

"Salaam, Kamla—it does look like a good mail, doesn't it? Thank you. Lots of nice things to read while Sahib is away." And off he swung on the bicycle to deliver the mail to other fortunate families, little realizing what he had left behind in my hands: an official-looking envelope from the church headquarters.

My husband was away in another part of India in meetings. This was often the case now that he was executive secretary of the Evangelical Fellowship of India, and so it became necessary for me to sort his mail, looking after matters that needed immediate attention. I looked at the envelope a long time before I dared open it, for I felt that heavy, ominous sensation that sometimes preceded news of a crisis sort.

I reached for the letter opener on my husband's desk and read the contents—my heart beating wildly as the meaning of what I read broke over me. I wished I could put it back into its envelope and seal it up, not only to shut up the envelope permanently, but to put the words I had read out of my mind—but this I could not do.

Would my husband even consider the offer to return to America as superintendent of our supporting church? I hoped not, but it was for him to decide. I tried to forget the whole thing. It would be days before he returned. There was no way to reach him, no way to share the news or the burden of it, no way to find assurance that this letter would not alter our lives or work in India.

I could not forget. The possibility of the dreaded upheaval was stamped upon my spirit, and as I turned to look out on that cloudless October day, a cloud of an inner sort settled upon my spirit.

Never had the orchard looked so promising. There were oranges and grapefruit, lemons, mangoes, figs, and guavas—trees we had bought as tiny saplings. We planted their roots deep into the ground and fertilized the earth around the roots with dead jackals and other wild animals as well as various of our pets that died, each with its own funeral, which the children morbidly conducted. Each tree was in a sense a marker for some unfortunate animal, and each tree gave promise of fruit in generous measure. It takes years to grow trees to the stage of yielding fruit, and I looked with pride and hope at the orchard we had rescued from the jungle.

The orchard was symbolic of the twenty-odd years in India during which so much had to be put in order to get any fruit at all. It was this kind of fruit that was so priceless and so full of hope, and I wanted to taste the fruit of our labor.

The letter made me feel very temporary and as though our precious and priceless years might slip away to an abrupt end. It seemed to me inevitable that we would have to go, perhaps because of the strange sadness I felt when the mailman brought the letter. My heart and my prayers cried out, "Please not now! Let this cup pass." But day after day brought further indications that we would have to let others reap what we had so hopefully sown and planted.

Dear Lord,

I relinquish that from which
I saw so little fruit.

The cause, I cannot say;
Perhaps no root?
Or was it toil unskilled
Or just that Thou hast willed
That I not know
What plant should grow?

Yet, keep Thou me from unbelief.
Perhaps a darker hand than mine
Will cut the sheaf
I might have brought,
And seeking, find the ones
For whom I sought.

When day is done
I ask but this
That they be won;
My crowning bliss
That I may clasp the darker hand
In joy complete,
That we may kneel together
At Thy feet.

I began unconsciously to say little farewells, first of all to nature, which had always spoken to me in parables. There were the birds, flitting about in the garden as they always had; I had become very much aware of their presence. For one thing, birds in India press their presence upon one by insistent calls and noisy conversations among themselves. Some sang a welcome tune to which I stopped to listen. Some chattered, some shouted, and some commented quietly as they hopped about among our potted plants, and some teetered unsteadily back and forth too embarrassed to say anything.

Color was another attention catcher—brilliant greens of barbets, red and blues of the blue roller. The size of birds, long white ribbon tails of the paradise fly catcher, the huge beaks of the hornbills could scarcely go unnoticed. Thus birds had become personal friends, and my acquaintance with the feathered friends had become a special tonic to me during the rains, and especially when the depression from too much of too much had entered my spirit.

How does one say goodbye to these charming little gifts of nature that had brought so much cheer and wholesomeness? Among the bird communities, they have their clowns, their artists, their homemakers, their thieves, and their policemen, their beauty queens, their royalty, and such blabbermouths as the babblers, for instance. They have their whiners and the "cheerer-uppers" and their tailors sewing a fine seam for their nursery needs. There are the lazy and the hard workers, the renters and the builders, the hoarders and spendthrifts. They are a charming community, and the thought of leaving them was a sad one indeed!

They (the birds) along with the orchard perhaps were only a symbol of the people who were most precious of all. The years of joyous labor and acquaintance had led to priceless fellowship that made leaving like tearing flesh from bone.

With October came also the camping season, and I thought surely we would spend most of the winter in the villages as usual. If it must be my last, it must certainly be the best, but already the decision to leave India proved valid. The evangelistic work was now in the hands of the Indian church, and we were invited to go with their camping parties, or not, as the need was felt. However, conditions had so changed and the anti-foreign propaganda was so damaging that our motives were questioned and characters maligned when American women appeared in the village. I was glad, then, that the book for village preaching that I had written could be put in the hands of Indians to use where we could no longer go.

We turned our attention to strengthening the existing churches, to all-India evangelism, and to conferences for Christian workers in India, and there were openings for such service in other neighboring countries.

When summer came we went once more to the Himalayan foothills to pack our things and sell what was left over. Mary now was the only child we had in boarding school. Always before I had gone down the mountain torn and heartsick, leaving one or more of my children in school. This time we would all go together. It would be the end of the second generation of boarding school separations. I did not know then that there would be a third!

Very close friendships were formed in these summer months for parents as well as for children. I knew now how Mother had felt about her missionary friends. I, too, had experienced the fellowship of Bible studies in our home as we met weekly together, and I remembered Father had done this in China.

Every Friday afternoon at Edge Hill was open house. Tea was served on the wide verandah that curved around the front of this boarding house. Special guests were invited, but anyone could come. There were dainty tomato sandwiches and cucumber sandwiches, and little cakes and tarts and curry puffs and cups of delicious tea served by the bearers (table boys) wearing white turbans and white knee length coats.

After tea there was a prayer meeting. The sitting room was filled with chairs to "squash" proportions for the service.

I loved these Friday services. They sang the hymns I was taught in the English school in Kuling. The room . . . the tea . . . the singing . . . the people who came there—all reminded me of my childhood when Mother took me to the China Inland Mission prayer meetings at Kuling. I felt closer to China in Landour than anywhere in India, and indeed it was just over the "white ridge" yonder, but those ridges rose to over 23,000 feet in places and made a sizable barrier that only imagination could cross, but I loved to look up at the eternal snows and watch them turn gold and pink with the sunset and sometimes silver when there was a full moon.

On the "snow" side of Landour, one was but a step away from fairy land, or China, or maybe even heaven!

On the "plains" side of the mountain, it was vastly different—the people's side where problems and heartache and the limitless sea of human need was so oppressive. We could see the plains far below and the thin wavy line of rivers growing farther and farther apart as they wend their crooked ways across the arid deserts and plains. Down there live the people, and somewhere 500 miles away are the half million living in the villages in one of the most backward parts of the subcontinent—my people. I loved them and had spent twenty-one years among them. It was now soon time to leave it all.

Landour was a place for me to think things out—suspended between the heights of inspiration and the depths of inadequate supply for the unending poverty below me.

As we came to the end of our last summer in Landour, I was invited by a dear friend to speak to a missionary group at a Friday prayer meeting in an English boarding house.

"Catherine," she said in her special English way, "you must come to Edge Hill on Friday and speak once again to our Friday prayer meeting."

"I really have nothing to say," I replied. "I have no message. Leaving India seems like not only the end of everything I had hoped for . . . actually, I think I am afraid to face going home. The truth is I have been disappointed in people who have left the field for home appointments. I am disappointed in ourselves. I believe in this work and want to see the fruit. What can I say to anyone? The future looks dark like a heavy cloud out there, and I feel sick at heart."

"You'll have a message for us; I'm sure of that. I'll put you down for next Friday," she said cheerily, and she left.

By Friday I had a message because I had found one for myself that was to make all the difference in my attitude about the months ahead.

The 139th Psalm was that message. As I read it to those missionaries, young and old, in Edge Hill that Friday, the presence of God was so real. I knew I would live by the words I was reading, and others started to live by them, too.

The words that were given to me that have followed me ever since were in the tenth verse:

> "EVEN THERE [in the past, present, or future] shall
> thy hand lead me, and thy right hand shall hold me."

Little did I know what these words, burning even at the time, were to mean to me in the weeks and months to follow. That it had been true I knew. I believed that it was true that very moment, and I was to prove its truth in whatever was behind the dark cloud that oppressed me, which I could only express in poetry.

SORROW'S PRAYER

Let sorrow have some meaning;
    Some lesson let it hold—
Some purpose in the heartbreak
    And the strain.
Let the darkening cloud above me
    And the thunder clap so bold
Be just the cloud which brings
    Refreshing rain!

Let all the dread of changes,
    The crisis we must meet,
Let all the pain of turmoil
    And the strife
Be but the pangs of travail
    The pain so bittersweet
Which ushers in a soul
    And gives it life!

And let the growing darkness
    And denseness of the night
Give way to purple streaks,
    To pinking grey,
To bring us to the daybreak
    And to a clearer sight
And to the happy dawning
    Of the day.

Chapter 10
Clouds

BACK ON THE PLAINS AGAIN the rains were breaking, but slowly. The clouds rolled black and lowering, and the heat was oppressive, and I felt again a strange heaviness. We packed all our things and shipped them to Calcutta.

What we could not take, we sold at auction, which is the way missionaries have settled upon to dispose of their belongings. To give them away causes jealousy. To put a value on them was arbitrary, and so they were sold at auction. I sat upstairs in the office and looked out of the window and saw my people out there in the courtyard bidding against one another for my precious things, however big or insignificant. They were really prizes and keepsakes to them—and I wept.

We left our home then—the Old Bungalow they called it. It was built for an American doctor years ago. It had been left vacant for years. When we went there, the jungle had crept up to the verandah—no yard, no orchard, no garden then. We found eight snakes in two weeks in and around the house. It was the only real home our children had known. We left it and went to live with my brother and wife, who were surgeon and nursing superintendent of our hospital, while other missionaries lived in "our" bungalow.

It was only a matter of days until we were to leave for America; we were awaiting the final word from the Annual Meeting in August.

The depression deepened as the days passed. Our first convert, whom we called our spiritual son, had defected. He had been offered a job by the Congress Party and in accepting it found himself unable to attend church or even to call himself a Christian. Little by little, after years of radiant witness, he had now even joined the opposition party headed by the son-in-law of an evangelist who had been dealt with by the church.

The evangelist had made many false promises to the villagers in order to make converts. The situation became menacing as villagers expected what was not possible. The man was dismissed, but his son-in-law saw a chance for a lawsuit. He talked to a party of Hindus who were particularly anti-Christian and antiforeign. The party had been building strength as the Congress Party had weakened, and lawyers among them jumped at the opportunity to embarrass the mission. There was a great deal of talk, and the young son-in-law was able to gather malcontents and a few who were easily led until the breach in the church was easily discernible.

What a time to leave—when the church was torn over the discipline of the preacher and the city was becoming involved and even the converts were shaken! How could this be when we had been given so many promises of "fruit [that] should remain" time and time again? Only a short time ago the work was so promising, such a thrill to see the Acts of the Apostles reenacted in the village of Bundelkhand.

But the government was cracking down—no missionaries were now allowed to make converts. In the last two years I had not been able to go to the villages except on rare occasions. In preparation for this time, the work had already been turned over to the Indian Church. I knew that this was very large in my husband's thinking when he decided to leave. He knew we would not be able to work freely as before, that if the Indian Church was to carry the responsibility of its own affairs and its evangelistic efforts, we would have to decrease and that the only way it could come about was to actually leave—not only leave it in their hands—but for us to leave the scene. I knew we could not stay on there. The handwriting was on the wall.

One day when we were walking from the Old Bungalow to the hospital, a secretary of the court came by on a bicycle and stopped, "Sahib," he said to my husband, "you are soon to be arrested for a criminal offense for defaming the character of your former preacher. The pastor of the church [an Indian] and the clerk of the Monthly Meeting are also to be arrested. Sahib, I have come at great risk to warn you. You are leaving soon anyway. Please leave right away. You cannot be involved if you are out of the country. If you stay and are arrested—you know Indian courts move slowly—you may be caught for years. There are all sorts of charges against you. None of them are true. But there are signed witnesses—some of them your friends. Please listen to me and leave. It would be a great sorrow to your true friends to see you so humiliated."

The leaders of the church were to be put under arrest, charged with defaming the character of a man who had been disciplined by the church. In India defamation of character is a criminal rather than a civil charge. The reason why Everett felt he could not leave his Indian brethren alone to face these charges was that implicit in the case was the issue of the right of the church to discipline its members. As such, the case gained India-wide attention.

The next day at noon while the four of us were eating lunch, the servant came in, terror stricken. "Sahib," he said to my brother, "the police are here."

"I will go," he said.

He went out and greeted the police in a friendly way.

"Oh, Doctor Sahib, please do not trouble. It is Cattell Sahib we want and your Indian pastor and male nurse [the Monthly Meeting clerk]."

"What do you want with them?"

"We have come to arrest them."

"What are the charges?"

"Defamation of character."

My brother returned, white and shaken. Frances, his wife, read his face and started weeping. "This is it, Everett. They have come for you."

He jumped up, wiping his lips carefully with his napkin, and went out.

"Here I am. I'll go with you to jail," he said briefly.

"Oh, no—no—Sahib—don't come." And to my brother, "Please go bail for him."

"Why should he go bail for me? If you want to arrest me, take me to your jail."

"But we have no place to keep you. We have no arrangements for keeping sahibs. Just please stay here until the trial. It would be very troublesome to have to arrange for your food."

"Well, you must think of those things when you go around arresting people." Just enough humor to help.

"Sahib, we are sorry to do this. These are our orders. Doctor Sahib, please help us out of this fix and go bail for him." Laughter flitted across our hearts for a moment.

By that time the Indian men were rounded up and bail was accepted for all three, and the dark clouds that had hung so close and ominously broke and the rains came.

My husband, always threatened with trouble in the veins of his legs, now was having his ulcerated leg treated. It was unusually bad, and the hot sultry weather did not help matters. The next day after the arrest, my sister-in-law reported typhoid fever in the hospital. Rebecca Coleman, who with her husband Milton now lived in the Old Bungalow—came down with typhoid also. She was very ill.

Mary was with us and the idea of her father being arrested by people she had thought were her friends disturbed her. She was too young to understand and too old not to feel the tenseness and heartache.

The loyal church members were shocked into action and rallied about the three men. Prayer meetings were called for the men on trial, for the women who were ill, for the village converts whose leader had defected.

The doctor was concerned about Mary. Living so close to typhoid in that hot, fly-ridden, sticky weather was not safe for her. There was nowhere to go. She should not have been there in this weather—school had opened again in Landour—but her place was taken and now we had no idea whether we could go to America in months or years as her daddy was caught in the trial. She had already lost too much schooling. Something had to be done.

Oh, how I needed the *hand to lead me and the Right Hand to hold me!* And It was there.

It became clear to all of us that this trouble spot was no place for Mary.

"Go to Jhansi," my husband said. "Go and help Anna Nixon at the EFI office and get Mary out of here. Doc and Frances will look after me. I'll be living there anyway. You must go."

Chapter 11
Cloudburst

JHANSI IS OUR NEAREST BIG CITY. We had to go to Jhansi whenever we went to the hills to get the train or to Bombay or anywhere at a distance. We went there to shop and for missionary union meetings, and we had friends there.

The person chosen to take over the EFI office from my husband was a young Assemese, Ben Wati, trained in America. He had lived with us and was much like a son to us. He and his wife and two daughters lived in Jhansi as also did Anna Nixon of our mission, a dear friend, who with Ben Wati carried on the work on an all-India basis that my husband had laid down.

Anna had taken my cook earlier in the month when I broke up housekeeping; so Ramzani, my faithful Mohammedan cook, was there was also Mary's Bai ji (*ayah*) who fortunately also had found a position there on the same compound. Mary was delighted to be back with her dearest servants and Auntie Anna, and the terror of events in Chhatarpur seemed less violent. We arrived the first day of August, which was her eleventh birthday, and she was surprised that night with a birthday party at Ben Wati's.

I worked in the office when Anna needed me and wrote letters and helped entertain the constant stream of guests who came and went. We were there a week. I was cut off from home and the happenings there, but word came that the first trial was set for August 8. I was very restless and clinging hard to my verse, wishing I could help at home, but knowing Mary needed me.

I went down to the office the morning of the eighth: sending letters to pastors all over India, folding these messages of encouragement and inspiration, and then enclosing them in thousands of envelopes.

Ben looked up from his desk. "Mrs. Cattell, do you believe in dreams?"

"Oh, I don't know. Why?"

"I want to know. Do you believe in them?" firmly.

"Well, Joseph did. I am sure some of them have a meaning, but some of them are influenced by mincemeat and hot spices. Do *you* believe in them, Ben? And why are you so serious about it?"

"I had one."

"Bad one?"

"Very bad."

"What was it?"

"That I would never tell."

"Come on, Ben, tell me. I like to hear about dreams."

"Mrs. Cattell, you would not like to hear about this one."

"Don't say that, Ben; this is the morning of the trial."

"It has nothing to do with the trial."

I shuddered and wondered.

Just then a servant from the big house on the hill came running into the office. "Memsahib, a car from your mission has just arrived and they are calling for you."

"All right," I said, "I'll be right there."

What could have happened to bring people to Jhansi on the day of the trial? Perhaps, oh, please, God, may it be that the trial has been dismissed. It will be good news. The thought brought conviction that surely my husband and the men were free. Lightheartedly, I ran into the great long sitting room of the upper house of the Canadian Presbyterian Mission.

There sat my husband, my brother, and my sister-in-law. Frances was weeping. Hope died as quickly as it was born. This was not good news.

"Sit down; we have sad news for you," said my husband. "David, Jane, and the baby have all been killed in a terrible accident."

David killed—how could he be dead? He is so vibrant—so full of life—I did not hear what they said about the others. I just could not believe that David could be dead.

"Jane?"

"She, too."

"Dead?"

"Yes."

"The baby?"

"The baby, too."

How could I believe such a thing? I could not take it in. Married a year. We had never seen the baby, and now all dead.

I looked about the room. There stood Ben. He had hurried up the hill following behind me. He knew.

"Ben—is this what you saw in your dream?"

"Yes—exactly."

Things came very clearly to me now. The fog and heaviness of the past six months were gone. It had been a slow preparation for this blow. The clouds had been drained. I knew I had to go back with them, my husband, my brother, and his wife, taking Mary. We would have a memorial service there with our people. They loved David. David was the friend of those who were now causing our deep sorrow. They had betrayed us, but they had loved David.

Riding back that lovely sun-drenched evening, crossing the swollen rivers on the ancient ferry boats, riding back the familiar way we had come so often, I felt a Hand holding me, and I said to myself, "Yes, even here!"

I had not been riding long when suddenly four sentences as clear as to be almost audible came to me.

There is a right way to handle grief—

Do not talk about this all the time.

Do not refuse to talk about it or make others shy of mentioning it.

Do not dramatize this experience in any way.
Do not ask me, "Why?"

I repeated these sentences aloud to my brother.

"That is the best advice I ever heard. Do what you are told," he said.

I felt four walls around me protecting me.

I have never felt the compulsion to tell everyone about the experience, but I have used it again and again when others have been called upon to face sudden sorrow of that kind. In this day when so many mothers have had to lose their sons, I have felt the bond between us and been able to reach out with the words God gave me—strong words—but right words that one can live by.

I have heard people scream into God's face, "Why? Why me?" and I thank God that He forbade me to ask it. Somehow that one question leads to bitterness and self-pity and sometimes to unbelief. I would *never* have known that!

Back at the mission, the full impact of what had happened began to dawn. Word had come to us four days after the accident. It was, in fact, on the day of the funeral when those three lifeless bodies were laid to rest that we learned of their death.

My husband, who had been excused from the trial when the news came by cable, was now standing for hours before the Hindu lawyers, heckled and maligned, suffering the pain of his ulcerated leg.

I heard that our spiritual son Khuba had signed that he would witness to several lies. One was that the sahib, my husband, had furnished munitions to the robber bands of the area; another, that he had paid people to become converts.

I sent for Khuba. "Tell him only that David has died with his wife and child, and I want him to know."

He bicycled the four miles early the next morning—a very chastened and troubled man.

"Khuba," I said, "I want you to know that I have lost two sons—David, who was my physical son, is dead—you, who were our spiritual son, are dead also; and my husband is now at your mercy."

He wept and said, "Memsahib, someday I will do the work of David and me both. He was my true brother. I will come back."

The women whom I had accepted years before as "my people" now came and sat on the floor with me in silence weeping, now and then remembering something about David. I thought of Job whose friends came to philosophize and sit with him in his grief. I had gone to these women when they had lost their children—it was tragically common in India. This was our last missionary assignment.

"You have taught us to believe.

"You have taught us to pray and to be better mothers.

"Today you are teaching us to suffer."

Suffering is a ministry and not a morbid one. I did not know that either. It is part of life like darkness is and clouds are. They have an important use. What a tragedy that sorrow should become the cause for bitterness when it was meant like rain for fruitfulness!

And now David was gone—Jane and the baby—all gone. They would never come now, but surely in the crisis of these our last weeks in India, their death surely had some relation to all this. Surely his friends would remember—surely Khuba, his special friend, would; but now he was about to witness lies against David's father. What a situation to climax twenty-one years in India! And just to think that David and his little family had sincerely hoped to return to India in another year—and things seemed to be working out at last.

So, I called Khuba the morning after we heard of David's death and I could see he was *remembering*. "Khuba," I said, "I know you are remembering David and his childhood here, but have you forgotten God? Have you forgotten the miracles you have seen with your own eyes?"

"No," he replied brokenly. "I have not forgotten anything. I will prove that I have not."

No word had come through as to the details of the accident or the funeral—where, how—and it was days before we did hear. But as we waited, a letter came from David himself—with the first pictures of his little daughter Lisa and his wife Jane. The letter was full of a proud father's description of the baby and of all that had happened. He had traded his car for a safer (?) one. He was full of plans for a vacation to begin Monday, which was to be the day after the accident on Sunday. He and the little family planned to meet us as we arrived in the States. In the letter he enclosed a very long list of things he wanted us to bring from India—including many local items of food and trinkets from the village.

When our Indian friends read the list they were deeply moved. These requests of simple village things proved to them that he had really loved them. The list and parts of his letter were read at his memorial service.

The Maharajah came to call on us to express his deep feeling for David, as also did the villagers. People who had been taking sides on the issues of the trial now were embarrassed, as also were the city officials who came to call.

The trial proceeded, however, as the three men were arraigned before the Hindu judge. The opposition had seven lawyers with piles of law books stacked in front of them. We had one lawyer. He also was a Hindu and very much wishing we would hire a few more lawyers to support the case.

"What is our story going to be?" he inquired.

"The truth. We do not need a story. We will just tell the truth, exactly as it was."

The lawyer was visibly terrified. "The truth—that's all? I have never conducted a case before with just the bare truth! You must have a good story."

Each day the lawyer met with the three men as they shared fresh promises from the Bible and had prayer for deliverance from evil men.

The lawyer was fascinated and intrigued. "What promise do we have from the Bible today?" he learned to ask.

As my husband's leg became worse—for long standing was the worst treatment it could have—and as the trial became more abusive, my brother Ezra went to court and stood beside the three men to the great embarrassment of the whole court.

"Doctor Sahib—please sit down. You are not on trial. Here is a chair—do be seated."

"I stand with the accused," he replied.

"The doctor must be treated with respect. Who knows when one of us might need him? Too bad he insists upon involving himself in this disagreeable situation," they said.

And now after the memorial service, Frances, the doctor's wife, my sister-in-law, came down with typhoid. We were living in her home. What to do now with Mary? It was getting near time for our flying date. There was no way of knowing if we would be able to leave soon or be delayed for months. The heavy baggage was all in Calcutta waiting. We could not send it on, as the final word from the home church would not be given until Yearly Meeting, the third week in August. If our return was affirmed by the vote there, we would leave the following Monday morning. If not—the whole thing would be cancelled and we would have to remake our plans.

The days were spent in trial and care of the sick. At night we sat about making and unmaking plans. To leave with Mary or not to leave—and where? I did not want to arrive in America if Everett was to be detained a long time in India. We had no home; Mary had no place in school in India. The time had come for some move.

About that time some of the missionaries began to come from stations round about to give what help and support they could. Upon hearing of the dilemma, one said, "Even God can't guide a ship tied to the wharf. Get moving. Start going and let God open or shut doors."

This made sense to all of us. I would start with Mary toward my other brother in Taiwan. We would stay there where schools would be available if we were delayed long, waiting for the trial.

It was decided, and once again Mary and I were on our way alone, and once again came those priceless words, "*Even there* shall thy hand lead me, and thy right hand shall hold me."

Leaving my husband in such distress of body and troubled in spirit, my sister-in-law ill with typhoid as also was Mrs. Coleman, the church torn, our son and family having been killed—could anyone imagine such a time to leave? My whole being cried out to stay and see it through and pitch into the challenge, but everyone felt I should try to go and let the Lord work out the details.

I walked down to the Old Bungalow to see my dear friend who was so ill and to say goodbye; and then I walked around the house, climbed the circular stairs to the roof, looked out over Bundelkhand—the villages barely visible, the compound so full of memories, so full of hope—and I wept.

"O God, this is your work, your people. Your name is at stake. We came at your call. We go at your leading; we suffer when you permit, but we claim victory. This is not the end. There will be fruit and it shall remain."

Letters began to arrive from America. Before Mary and I left the mission station, we had been able to put the bits and pieces of information together giving us as a family at least some idea of what had happened. It was cruelly simple, one of those things that should never have been; a previous accident had knocked down a stop sign on a strange road, with cornfields hiding the crossroad over the crest of the hill.

The funeral was at Jane's home church and the burial there also. Barbara, our married daughter, and her husband John had taken care of our end. She chose our special family hymns, "Be Still, My Soul" and "Great Is Thy Faithfulness." The man whom we would have chosen had the service, the only other man in our China mission beside my father—Dr. Walter Williams. He helped us when Father had died there when we were children, and he was there now to lay our son and his family to rest. He had married David and Jane the year before. Jane's family had been especially brave and strong. They were a marvel to all who came to the funeral. It was infinite comfort to us to know this.

Everything had been done, and just as we would have done it, but it all seemed so unnecessary. But I dared not tread on that ground. It led right up to "Why?" and this was forbidden.

What infinite wisdom in those four sentences I did not realize at the time, but looking back I can see that to ask why would have been to open the door of doubt and endless questions for which there was no answer on this side of heaven. There was a reason. There had to be a purpose, and for a little family to suddenly enter the presence of God should not be thought of as tragedy, not if we believe anything of what Christ taught us about going to prepare a place.

I realized that only as my heart was quiet could I feel His right hand holding me.

One evening as we were sitting together trying to adjust our minds to what had happened, my brother Ezra said, "Perhaps it is like twins in a mother's dark womb—warm, safe and secure, but dark. One of them is born and temporarily precedes the other in life outside in the wonderful new world of light. The one left behind wonders what terrible thing may have happened to the twin, only to follow shortly himself to see that life in this new world is far better than what was known before." The thought brought great comfort to all of us and I clung to this illustration.

It seemed incredible that I would have to leave my husband with no end of the trial in sight. To leave him there to suffer humiliation and abuse in court seemed an added cruelty. His leg was painful and getting worse. I hated to leave my sister-in-law ill, the mission torn, the object of scorn and all of India watching. It just did not seem right to go and yet it was agreed by missionaries, Indians, and all, that this was the best plan, best for Mary surely, and perhaps even best for early dismissal of the trial if people could see we had confidence to carry on the original plan. If it was not right, we trusted God to stop us before we left India.

One hot August day Mary and I started for Calcutta.

The missionary family is a large one. We reached out to one another. In a backward area where there were neither motels, hotels, nor restaurants, our homes became hostels for each other anywhere in India. I had had my share of moving over and making room for all kinds of people—the choice souls from all over India, visitors from America and many other countries. It is just one of those things one does. The first things we offer are a hot bath and a hot cup of tea and a place to lie down. Nothing was too much trouble when help was needed, and in this our hour of need, no trouble was too much for our friends.

We were taken into the Corlett home in Calcutta. Walter Corlett was pastor of Carey Baptist Church, and they lived at the manse where William Carey himself had lived. Here was English hospitality at its warmest and best. Here we were given every consideration. Violet Corlett took Mary and me up and down, in and out the twisting crowded streets of Calcutta to start the unwinding of red tape to get a new passport for the two of us instead of three. The ticket had to be changed. There were endless offices to find, papers to fill out, people to see. The plane was leaving early Monday morning.

Never have I seen a church used as Carey Baptist. There was a program on constantly. It served as a Bible school, a youth center, a church for English, church for Bengali, and in the afternoon on Sunday church for the Chinese. On Sunday the pastor asked me to bring the message for this service. It was my final Sunday in India, and I was given the privilege of preaching to my beloved Chinese in the church made famous by William Carey as the founder of modern missions in this my adopted land.

That night a missionary friend said to me, "Let there be no *if only*!" Don't let your mind be tormented by wondering how things might have been different if only you had done this or that. David was *not*, for God took him."

I have seen people so tortured by this very thought that hinges on an *if only*, and I thank God for sparing me from tormenting thoughts I know I would have had, had I not been warned.

Chapter 12
Island Beautiful

Monday morning came and with it the departure from India with Mary Catherine, leaving behind me my husband, "my people," the wonderful family of missionaries—and carrying with me a nameless ache and great uncertainty. Just before the flight was announced, an Indian evangelist came in to the airport. We talked a little and he prayed for Everett and the trial, for Mary and me in our flight. He handed me a telegram of farewell from the leaders of the Evangelical Fellowship of India, and it was time to go. How comforting was the presence and the prayer of this Indian brother! I remember when I saw the plane poised for takeoff, we climbed in and fastened seat belts, those words came to me: *If I take the wings of the morning . . . behold, Thou art there.*

In a matter of hours, we were in Rangoon met by dear friends from China in the days when Karis and I were in Shanghai American School together. She had been the oldest of our "eightsome." Today she was opening her arms and her home to me and my daughter in Burma.

Rain was pouring down, and all the plans to see Rangoon resulted in spending those precious hours in the loving care of a girlhood friend. God knew that a touch of China and early memories would be a balm to my torn and troubled heart.

The next day we arrived in Hong Kong. This was China—real China. I thought I knew no one there although it had originally been planned that Everett would have been the speaker at the Hong Kong Keswick, which was in session at the time.

I felt I should at least drop in. I went—and the rain poured, but when I got to the church, there were missionaries who had heard about the sorrow we were experiencing and were praying for us. Our situation was brought before the Lord in public prayer with hundreds of Christians in loving concern, and suddenly my faith began to grasp the promise again, "Yes—even here."

My brother and his wife met us in Taipei, my own brother Charles, with members of the Chinese church and other missionaries at the airport. Along with them was an elderly man, short, dignified, and we noticed that he was in the very center of the Chinese delegation to meet us. When our suitcases had passed the customs inspection and we were really in Taipei, free to move about, we were introduced to the gentleman. The story was this: his daughter had been a roommate of our David's wife. It was to visit her that our little family were traveling on that day when, suddenly, they were struck by an oncoming car. The visit to the girl from Taiwan was never made, but the father heard of this proposed visit and was in deep mourning with us.

"Charles," I said to my brother, "please take me somewhere to rest. I do not feel up to meeting a lot of people."

"No, that cannot be. It does not fit in with our plans," he replied, in his familiarly authoritative way. "You are expected at one of our churches tonight and they will expect to hear a few words from you."

"Me? Speak tonight?"

"Oh, yes," he added, "and tomorrow at a luncheon there will be a large crowd of missionaries from the upper half of the island who are in the city now waiting to hear from Everett on the Evangelical Fellowship of India. I think you will have to bring the message and tell what you can of this fellowship and its work."

I was thinking of sputtering some objection, until the words came gently to my mind, "Never mind; even there."

The next day seated at the head table beside my brother and the leading missionaries of the island, just before I was introduced as the speaker to take my husband's place, the same gentleman we had met at the airport came walking up from the back of the room past the tables where guests were seated, on up to the head table, carrying a basket of red roses tied with black ribbon. With it was a letter of deep regret that the attempt to befriend his daughter should have robbed us of our only son. An explanation was made to the visitors of this touching gesture.

Ah, it was the Chinese who knew how to enter into this sorrow. It was he who pointed out that there would be no one to carry on the family name. Sooner or later we would have thought of that aspect, but coming from this Chinese gentleman, somehow done with such understanding and love in this public act of recognition, I could only think that only God could have thought of this beautiful way of providing comfort. It was easy after that to speak to these kind and gracious people.

The Chinese have suffered. Those from the mainland have lost their relatives, scattered here and there, torn from their homes and roots to individually escape if escape they could. The women who had lost their sons in the war stood before me, not weeping, only reaching out to me with understanding.

After ten days of visiting churches and looking about, meeting new friends, the time came for the dedication of a new church. It was a very big affair with a church-wide feast. Orchids decorated the church and baskets of other exotic flowers. I sat on the platform to represent my husband, for the new appointment from the home church was general superintendent. This had implications on the mission fields, and he was to have been present at this special occasion. So, while he was back in India, on trial before a Hindu court, I sat in the seat of honor in his place.

The front door was opposite to me and it was open so that I could see out into the street. During the singing of a hymn, I saw a man on a bicycle stop, get off, and hold a yellow envelope in his hand. My brother saw him, too, and rushed from the platform out to the door; he bowed; the telegraph man bowed and handed him the envelope. I watched it all, and I knew in my soul that the cable was for me and it bore news of the trial. Good news or bad, I was soon to know. My brother tore it open and announced to the audience that Everett was acquitted along with our Indian brothers and that Everett was on the way to Taiwan to join Mary Catherine and me!

The dedication service now was a celebration of great joy, and the church entered into my joy as it had into my sorrow, and I rejoiced with them in their day of dedication, a new lighthouse from which the Gospel would be preached.

Never had a court case, especially on a criminal charge, been dismissed so quickly. In seventeen days the court convened thirteen times—a record breaker! It was a cause for great rejoicing in all India inasmuch as many missions and many non-Christians were watching to see what would happen. It was a great victory for the church, but victory came at a tremendous price as is often the case. We did not know then that a series of appeals would be made that eventuated in the Supreme Court of Madya Pradesh Province giving a resounding decision in favor of the church after three years of frequent trials.

In Taiwan there was rejoicing as my husband was able to join us there and in America as well. What appeared to be indefinite delay in Everett's new assignment was actually only one week late. Of course the prolonged preaching missions in Hong Kong, Saigon, Japan, and the Philippines were scratched; but everywhere there was great rejoicing over the result of those trying and heartbreaking days.

Again, "Great Is Thy Faithfulness" seemed the most appropriate hymn to suit our thanksgiving.

I was utterly amazed that there were on the island and in our churches some of the people whom I had known as a child in China. One day we visited Betty Chen, whose mother was the very one I claimed as my Chinese sister in Luho many years before.

Riding on the Taiwanese trains I wondered, "Can this be the East?" The trains were prompt and clean; music was piped into the cars; tea was served hot each hour, food vended

—such delicious Chinese food to eat with chopsticks right on the train. Hostesses in trim blue uniforms and hats looked like our air hostesses. This was a strange version of the East to me. Indian trains were a mass of squirming and crowded humanity with every man for himself, but here they were advanced indeed.

I was surprised in this atmosphere that my brother would speak so loudly that every passenger in the car would be able to hear him. His Chinese rang out over the music and all other sounds. Being his sister for some time, I felt free to chide him about all this unnecessary loud talk in such otherwise genteel surroundings.

"How do you suppose we have found so many of our original Luho Christians, students, former patients, and their children? People from Luho County have a dialect quite distinctly their own, and when people from there hear it, they know that here is a man from home; we have been able to join families and gather our former friends and members. Even those who were not Christians, torn as they are from their roots and loved ones, are in a receptive mood for the Gospel."

I sat amused to myself. "So God can use even loud voices on trains and in public places to gather His kingdom!"

Life in the East came abruptly to an end the day we arrived in the Chicago airport, the three of us. We rushed to the rest rooms to freshen up, searching through our bags for something suitable to wear upon arrival in the Ohio town where Everett's mother and sisters and our Barbara and her husband and baby daughter were to meet us. It had been less than six weeks since news of David's accident and death had reached us in India, and it was preeminently apparent in the small gathering waiting at the airport to receive us that he who had so eagerly awaited our return was not there. The little family *was not, for God took them.*

There was such a confusion of emotion within us as we greeted the church leaders who were there to give us official welcome! It was so wonderful to see Barbara and her little girl, Jeannie. There were to have been two little granddaughters, but only Jeannie was there and so dainty and precious. Our tall son-in-law stood there so capable and strong. There was weeping and joyous laughter. There were warmth and formal handshakes; and then we were whisked away to the home of a dear friend in the little town that is the center of evangelical Quakerdom in Ohio.

Sorrow lingered, heavy at times, as a backdrop to all that we experienced from day to day of challenge, of the new responsibility of leadership in the West, of great kindness, of great joy—and of deep gratitude for deliverance from the arrest, which very well could have turned out much differently!

The adjustment and the tumult of emotion was hardest for Mary Catherine. She was already late for the opening of school in September, but by the time she graduated from the eighth grade, she tied for the distinction of being the most outstanding girl in school.

Upon our return to America, Mary Catherine's health problems increased, and she has had to contend with them ever since. She has learned to live with them, and her experience of knowing suffering firsthand, her love for people regardless of color or race have given to her a depth that is rare and an understanding that has made her very successful in her teaching profession. Her special gift lies in motivating the underprivileged, both black and white, and loving them into striving for better things.

Mary Catherine and her husband, Fred Boots, a Columbus, Ohio, Friend, have a lovely home—Chinese art in the living room and Indian treasures in the guest room. Thus, adding together sorrow, suffering, and her life in India, her life has been enriched, and through her the lives of many high school students who had little to challenge them.

At the close of a year teaching in an all black high school in Georgia, the song, "Bridge over Troubled Waters," came over the public address system dedicated to Mrs. Boots with the explanation that she had been a "bridge" over the troubled waters of racial tension in the school.

Life in the West had begun in earnest. This was not a furlough. This was it! What was one to do with the twenty-one years in India? Forget them? Is there no continuity in life?

Ah, yes! Village life in India—its simplicity—its down-to-earthness made communication in the West possible, for we had learned to start with basics. Who was to know where life in America was to take us?

Never in our wildest dreams did we ever imagine we would in three short years be catapulted into a Friends college and that I was to be the wife of the president!

Life is whole and each part of it contributes to the next. We leave geography behind, but carry forever in our hearts the impact of other people, other experiences, other lessons learned under different skies.

We lived in America and gave ourselves to the needs and situations here, but India and China are forever a part of what we are, and we are richer—far richer for what life in the East has contributed to us.

The roots of the mango tree go very deep, searching for water far below the dry and arid surface. It is the depth to which it goes that makes it fruitful in adversity and fragrant when all else is dry, withered, and barren.

Scorching winds do not discourage a mango tree, nor do winds of adversity need to rob one of lovely fruit—not if the roots go deep enough.

India is the land of mangoes.

YESTERDAY AND TOMORROW

Yesterday, I came away
And left the known behind;
The bits of life of every day
Which slowly took a shape
And came to be
A part of me:
    Faces
    Places, etched in memory;
Wisps of sorrow; joys of a priceless kind;
Things of which I now am made
And offer no escape.

Yesterday, I came away
And left the past behind.

That is why I feel alone,
The past so vivid, how
Can I forget?
The future course
    Not set
    As yet,
I cannot guess the shape that it will find.
I only know my life today seems
Strange and not my own.

Between the past I knew
And tomorrow's unseen way,
Stands God, in faithfulness
With grace for my today.

Section IV
Epilogue

Once More Around

Epilogue
Once More Around

FOURTEEN WONDERFUL AMERICAN YEARS LATER, the opportunity came to revisit the Orient. We had only six weeks to spare, but they were enough to give us ten days in Taiwan, ten days at our mission in India, and a week for the conference in South India where Everett was to speak to the Evangelical Fellowship of India, which he had helped to found twenty years before.

China's doors had been closed for years to missionaries, but the island of Taiwan was wide open, and brother Charles and his wife were still there, still so close to the China of our childhood, still speaking the language and adopting its culture as always. However, now it was not as children adopting a culture but on a university level, as professor in botany. He had turned his childhood hobby into a Ph.D. and then into a professorship in the National University of Taiwan.

Our daughter Barbara, brought up in ways Indian, was with her husband John in their second term as missionaries in Taipei, and our four grandchildren with them. The littlest was a baby boy whom we had never seen. Our grandchildren were our third generation brought up in the Orient. It had been Mainland China, then India, and now back to a very miniature, up-to-date version of China again!

We arrived Christmas week, so the children were on vacation. The two older children, Jeannie and David, attended an American school in Taipei very like the Shanghai American School of our day; but, unlike us, they were able to live at home. Jonathan went to a missionary school much like Hillcrest in Nanking, but similarities were hard to find. Barbara's family lived in a Chinese house at the far end of the capital city—a house like all the other houses on the narrow street running along the canal. It was walled about, as all the houses were, each with a bright red gate. The house was small and the yard was smaller. I thought of the vast Quakerage yard in Nanking and our yard in Luho, where we had space to play and trees to climb; and yet this was the new day when missionaries no longer live the isolated lives of pioneers but mingle freely and live close to their Chinese neighbors.

Yet the standard of living is so much higher on the island. This is a very modern city, and our grandchildren came and went freely without the restriction of our early days, and they seemed happy in the hustle and bustle of the crowded city.

While I was adjusting myself to this most delightful and strange mixture of the familiar and the unexpected, the local pastor came to call. He brought me a length of beautiful peacock green brocade satin—a gift from all the Friends pastors and their wives. I was very touched. I found myself speaking a little in Chinese to him; and as I did, the words kept coming from somewhere back in the memory.

Along with the gift came the request that it be made into a two-piece Chinese dress immediately and worn on Christmas Day when the twelve Friends churches in the area were planning a celebration for the entire afternoon and evening with a Chinese feast between. It was to be a big affair with a thousand people expected. Where was one to find a tailor that could possibly turn out a fully lined dress in such a short time? The problem was quickly solved as Barbara knew of a shop advertising eight-hour service. Unbelievable, but it was true!

The evening of the next day Charles came into the room where I was rocking little Tim and said I was expected to be at a church seven miles away. I reluctantly left the baby, got ready to go with Charles and his wife Leora. It was raining a little as the three of us walked along to the bus stop. Chinese smells from little shops along the road awakened memories of many years ago. By night on the side streets I could really put myself back into old China.

Charles interrupted my reverie with, "Catherine, I am so glad you got here in time to celebrate this special night with me."

"This night?" I asked in confusion.

"It is the twenty-second of December, you know."

"Well, Mother died the twenty-second, but that was long ago," I remembered.

"How long?" asked Charles.

"I just can't say without counting up."

"Fifty years ago tonight. It was just fifty years ago that she rose up as she was dying and cried out, 'Who will go?' and you said you would, and I said I would, and here we are fifty years later, side by side, walking down a Chinese street together!"

I was deeply moved, not only at the memory and the realization that all three of us had gone—Charles to Taiwan, Ezra and I to India; but also this reunion on the very day. What perfect timing! Who but God could have arranged it and made it so meaningful?

Charles told this in church an hour later at the end of a long bus trip where the Christians were waiting for us. It had a profound effect on them. Nowhere are family ties and relationships more reflected and appreciated than in Taiwan, where refugees are lost from loved ones and family.

What would happen here? People were wondering, and one sensed great concern. Thousands had fled to the last possible refuge from communism. Thousands were also longing to get back to the Mainland. But who among us, or them, could foresee the tragedy that Taiwan would in the end lose her place at the UN? Where now?

In the face of all this the church was moving ahead. On Christmas Day the Christians belonging to our Friends churches came together, and we were deeply moved by the seriousness of their commitment, their enthusiasm, and by the quality of the people themselves. Many were government officers and families, some were professors, many were business people, and there were both Mainlanders and Taiwanese. They came from all walks of life—people willing to give their Christmas Day to fellowship and worship.

I wore the dress they gave me, and the women stood around to comment on the cut and style. I felt that they approved. Somehow I was able to summon enough Chinese to say a few words. It was strange to be coached by Barbara—now fluent in Chinese—whom we had brought up in India with Hindi as her first language.

Barbara has for some time given a ten-minute Gospel message twice a week to the officers' wives, for whom Madame Chiang has organized a sewing program to build morale. They were a somewhat captive audience and the Gospel was condensed into capsule form, as at the end of the allotted ten minutes the sewing machines began to roll whether or not the message was over.

Barbara asked me to accompany her when she gave the Christmas message to the group of over a hundred. I was introduced to the lady in charge as Barbara's mother—a visitor for Christmas, and it was mentioned I had been born in China.

I took my place behind a sewing machine to watch proceedings. Barbara got out the organ, pumped up the air and played, "Hark, the Herald Angels Sing," singing it with very little other participation. She was preparing to speak when the lady in charge introduced me to the crowd and mentioned my China background and then bowed to me saying, "She will now speak to you in Chinese!"

I had had no idea of speaking at all. In fact, I was sitting there impressed with the total lack of interest in the proceedings. There was no response, and I felt perhaps there was hostility to the whole idea of the service. I was terrified. What was I to do? I did not want to let anyone down, so I found myself standing up and starting to speak in Chinese:

"It is true I was born in China just as you were.

"It was my childhood home as it was yours.

"My father died in China and was buried there. Perhaps yours was also.

"I cannot return there, even as you cannot.

"I love China, and I love you."

I bowed and sat down.

They clapped. I had taken some of Barbara's total of ten minutes and wondered what she would do, but she came through with something very beautiful.

She said, "You must have known I had a mother. You may not have given it much thought. All you knew of my mother—what she is like—was whatever of her is in me. But today you have seen her and know her. You must know there is a God, although you may not have given it too much thought. What is He like? And there was no way we could have known until He sent His Son—the Son of God was born in this world and became man that He could lead us to God and show us what God is like."

It was great, and from there she gave the Christmas story in a few words and asked me to pass out the tracts on Christmas. "Pass them out with both hands," she said. So I did. The surprising thing was that the atmosphere was completely changed. There were smiles and some inquired where I was born. When I said "Luho, near Nanking" several began to chat, and we discovered neighbors and warm friends emerging from the hostility.

Barbara said it was her first breakthrough to personal response of any kind. The human element and family ties are so fundamental here where parents are left behind the Bamboo Curtain and children lost somewhere back on the Mainland. The hostility was bitterness from years of disillusionment and heartache.

This trip amazed me. God used relationships rather than sermons to soften hearts.

After the newness began to wear off, old China came through. There were moon-shaped doors, pagodas elaborately decorated, temples with gods and incense burning, men carrying baskets of vegetables on each end of a bamboo pole that rested on their shoulders.

There were old ladies wearing the black trousers. Some even had bound feet. Everywhere the clothshops were bulging with the brocade silks in most gorgeous colors. I was told that the color that had been given to me was the favored color for the new garments for China New Year's.

Upright signs with Chinese characters hung from every shop.

Yes, this was China—a sophisticated China, but China nevertheless; and on Christmas Day when Charles gave me a box of Mainland sweets like we bought off the streets of Luho when we were children, I knew I was home!

Christmas morning in China with my brother Charles and his wife Leora, in the home of our daughter Barbara and her husband and the four grandchildren, was priceless. There was such a pile of presents under the tree, whose only decorations were tiny lights. Endless gifts big and small, but at the very end of the gift-giving came the surprise that eclipsed all else!

Barbara showed us her passport, flight ticket, and all papers in order to go with us to India for ten days. John had conceived the idea, gotten permission from the home board, worked out all the details, and given her for her Christmas the trip to the land of her childhood with us! All arrangements were made for the children. There was not a single problem that did not find a satisfactory solution. It was the last day of the year when we flew off together to Hong Kong.

The island of Hong Kong was so close to Mainland China. I could see it—just on the other side of those mountains—those truly China mountains—the land of my birth! China's mountains are very beautiful. There is a quality about them, "pagoda-ed" and mysterious, peaceful, steep but not rugged, ageless but not barren, shrouded in mist.

We looked out upon China—so close and yet behind an invisible curtain, and yet there it lay before us, calling.

Not all of Red China is hidden behind the mountain. In Hong Kong itself there is a section reserved for Red Chinese flying their red flag from stores and homes.

As enemy land, this section has a dangerous and ominous feel. But to see the people there as people—individuals—that is different. I stood and watched a woman alone on her houseboat and wondered what she was feeling, what she was thinking. She sat and ate a bowl of rice with chopsticks. She threw

From left to right: Anna Nixon, Catherine Cattell, Norma Freer, Frances DeVol, Rebecca Coleman, Esther Hess, and Betty Robinson. Back row left to right: Everett Cattell, Ralph Comfort, Ezra DeVol, Linden Cole, Milton Coleman, Chester Stanley, Robert Hess, and Clifton Robinson.

Taipei, Dec. 10, 1971
Taken on Barbara's birthday

The naval officer (a Friend) holds the banner given to Everett and Catherine Cattell as they departed from Taiwan to India in 1971.

Brother Charles.

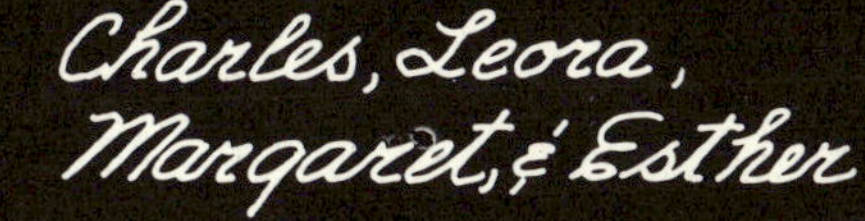

Ezra and Frances with Joe (left), Philip, and twins Priscilla and Patricia.

Dr. Ezra De Vol and assistants

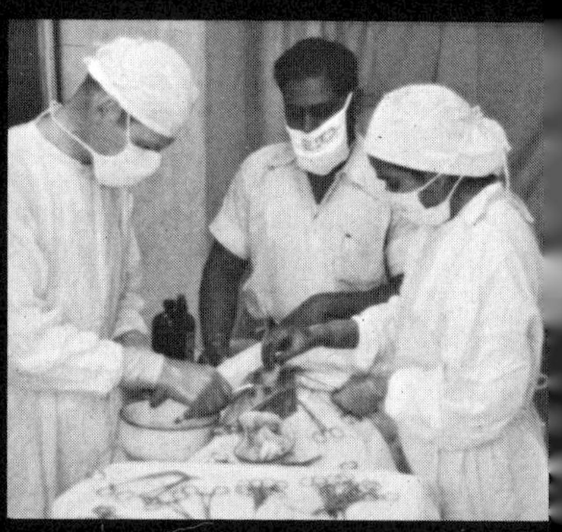

Ezra & Frances Joe & Phil in India

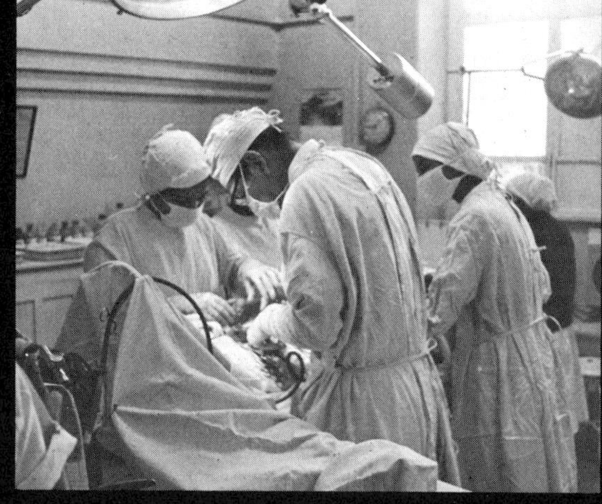

Dr. Ezra De Vol, surgeon; Frances De Vol, R.N.; and assistants

a morsel now and then to one and another of the three dogs beside her. She, too, must feel the need of protection. She had no way of knowing I loved her. She watched me for a little, then turned her back, and I moved on with the tour.

I pray that it will not be long before China will once more be open to the Gospel, that it may once more be a nation without the forbidding adjective—*Red.*

It was a wonderful New Year's Day sharing my China memories with Barbara, who now with her family was carrying on the China tradition.

By afternoon we left Hong Kong with its high rises, its apartment buildings bursting with humanity, clothes drying from bamboo poles, threaded through the sleeves of garments blowing in the wind from the windows of every floor. We left the shops standing cheek by jowl to modern stores, displaying priceless objects of art carved in ivory or jade. There were silks and brocades in the most irresistible designs and colors. There were lacquer screens with inlaid mother of pearl. It was all there—all the wealth of the ageless craftsmanship from behind the Bamboo Curtain.

More than anything that spoke of the China we knew were bamboo groves. If the dragon is one symbol of Chinese art, bamboo is the other, and much more practical. No tree stands so straight, so proud and so lovely, so delicate and yet so strong and so versatile. Bamboo was never meant to be a "curtain" to isolate a great nation. It is rather a hollow channel to carry LIFE to a languishing people!

It was night when we looked down from the plane and saw the lights of India beneath us. It had been eighteen years since Barbara left India to go to college—over thirteen years since we left it in the midst of such distress and sorrow. There was time enough for many changes to take place—and many changes had, both in India and in each of us; but we were struck rather by the familiar sights and sounds.

The cold of winter nights in unheated hostels, the crows screaming at our windows at dawn, the friendly birds in the garden where the *mali* worked about among the chrysanthemum plants, and watered the flower pots—this was India! People.

People. People. Coolies waiting, even fighting, for a chance to earn a pittance. So many people to do a single job! India has too many people.

New Delhi and the cities of India have indeed changed. High rises, new banks, hotels, wider streets, more cars and busses, and modern shopping areas—all these—and much more, show progress of a city, a nation perhaps, but at the railway station, we were back in the old India so familiar to each of us. People sleep huddled in corners here and there, or out on the station platform. The waiting room emits the usual strong smell of urine. The *ayah* still presides over the women's room with her tin can, ready to pour into it what she hopes will be left over in the teapots of passengers waiting between trains. Vendors still stalk the platform selling their wares: cigarettes, peanuts, bracelets, and fruit. Beggars are still begging, deformed, pitiful to see—some false poverty, some really in need. The platform more crowded than ever!

The night on the train was cold, sooty, and so, so familiar. Sleep was out of the question. In the early morning flying past fields, villages, wildlife, people, we sat silently each in our own thoughts remembering and overjoyed to be back home. We looked up and said to each other, "Did we ever go away? It is just as we left it."

India looks so very old. The land is worn out and almost desert, dotted with thorns and tormented with stones. The hills are rock heaps. The trees are old and gnarled and leaves are grey with dust . . . dust . . . we had forgotten about the dust, clouds of it rising, settling to rise again and again.

The welcome at the mission was very moving. After a brief service of garlanding and a prayer by the pastor, we fell into the arms of our people. Barbara had left as a girl. She returned as a woman. Her playmates were also women with families. She was one of them. There were nurses with whom she had worked one winter when she became a nurse's aide, looking for something to do while on vacation. She was filling in the years in between with the young women who had once been her chums. As it turned out, she had a unique ministry with the young folk of the mission, and now it was my turn to help her with her Hindi in which she was once so fluent!

Standing next to me was a village woman with a family of four boys and a girl. I had known her years before when she herself was a girl. She brought her family to me and introduced them. Her husband was a postman. One son was a technician; others were students in school. She looked up into my face and said, "I told you I would." And I knew what she meant; years before she made me the promise that she would one day be a Christian and win her family.

David was fifteen at that time. He and I went on bicycles to a village four miles away each Sunday morning. He took a branch from the mango tree and swept away the animal dirt from under it while I played the harmonium to let the people know it was time for service. People came from two nearby villages to this field, which belonged to this girl's father. She was so delighted to see us each Sunday, offering to help me or David wherever she could; and she listened very attentively. The men squatted on one side. The women sat on the other side of this outdoor service, and "Little Sister" took up the collection on a hymnbook, but she could not read. She did learn to sing the songs anyway, and after I preached, she came to me and hung on to my sari and, looking up into my face said, "When I grow up, I am going to be a Christian." It was against the law to make converts of children in that area. They could believe, secretly, but not confess Christ openly; but now here she was a mature woman, having brought up her family as Christians and having won two brothers and their families besides! I wonder if David knows this, that he has fruit in India. It was infinite comfort to me to know that he had a part in the work that is still going on in the villages he loved so much.

The last time I had attended a service in this church had been David's memorial service. While I felt him very near, this revisiting was one of great joy and reunion with those he had loved. Many a woman came to me in the week of our stay saying they too had lost loved ones—sons, daughters, husbands in these years; but they remembered the circumstances of our leaving and how God had sustained us, and they, too, had found God faithful to them in their need.

The one woman I would have loved to see was Mary Catherine's baby-sitter. I never called her *ayah.* She, as I have said earlier, was a real lady and a Christian, and Mary adored her. She died some time before our arrival. Mary wrote to her Aunt Frances, Ezra's wife, asking her to make a special floral arrangement and put it in the church in memory of Bai ji. This had not yet been done, so at the special Sunday morning service of Quarterly Meeting, Frances asked me to make a statement about the flowers and give Mary's message. It went like this:

"These flowers are in memory of Bai ji. I know that usually missionaries are expected to teach others about Christ and lead people to Him, but while my parents were doing this among you, Bai ji read Bible stories to me. She prayed with me and gave me a love for God. She, herself, was an example. I want to thank the Indian Church for their influence upon me, a missionary girl brought up in your midst, and I love you all even though I could not be with my parents and Barbara on this visit."

The entire church responded, standing to their feet in acknowledgment of her greetings and appreciation of her friends. The flowers were later given to Bai ji's daughters.

It was satisfying to me that the three of our children had each had a part in this return to India.

Ezra and Frances opened their home to us. Their son and his wife and two granddaughters were also visiting them for the Christmas vacation from Woodstock School, where he was teaching—so in India we had a wonderful family reunion, even as in Taiwan.

We visited the village where we had lived and taught, where Everett and our son David had been threatened and driven out of town years before, where also we had seen the greatest victories and miracles of God's protection and care.

The week was soon over. The house where we lived for seventeen years was empty—the orchard all but gone, the flower garden unattended, but the flowering trees there, the oleanders and hibiscus, and the temple tree we had planted. The mango trees were still there. It was no longer a lone house in the jungle. The neighboring land was used for farms now and houses were coming closer. Soon it would be a part of a growing city. It was more home to all of us than any other place on earth. We climbed up to the flat roof and looked out over the brown, dry countryside remembering the past and praying for "our people" who would soon be left behind again.

There is an airstrip thirty miles from this backward place where an ancient temple site has brought tourists from around the world to view its famous architecture of a thousand years. We took the plane from there and flew up over Bundelkhand, giving us for the first time a bird's-eye view of this countryside we love so very much. I wondered if we would ever see it again.

There was nothing below us but brown, rocky soil—dry, parched, and uncultivable except for a few patches of green. It is a perfect picture of the area spiritually—dry, hopelessly hard, and unproductive except for a few patches of green where new LIFE is giving hope of a real harvest.

Barbara and I exchanged our reactions to her "homeland" after eighteen years compared to how I reacted to China. It was a great visit. Barbara said that everything—the house, yard, hospital, church—were all smaller than she expected them to be, but the people, aside from loss of a few teeth and graying hair, were just exactly the same.

At Delhi again, Barbara returned to her "emerald isle" and to her little family and missionary work. We went on to South India to the Evangelical Fellowship of India Conference at Vellore, for which the trip was made. This day was goodbye to my brother and his family, our Indian friends of the mission, and to Barbara.

There were moments when India seemed to me so much as we had left it that it was as though we had never left—the dust, the village woman carrying heavy burdens on her head: of wood, waterpots, baskets of grain. There was the smoky smell of burning cow dung cakes rising up through the tiles of houses. Poverty was everywhere and cows still considered too sacred to kill, to use for food.

I looked again and it seemed a new India rising up before my eyes: new roads, bridges to span the rivers we once had to ford, busses to take place of lorries with board seats, and a modern gasoline station at the edge of town!

Most of all the changes were in the people. The orphans I had known were growing old. Their children were adults. Some were now professors in the local college. The educational standard within the church was so much higher. There were several who now carried heavy responsibility in the development of Christian literature, and in hospitals. Evangelists preached with power and inspiration. Leadership was no longer foreign. Even Indian missionaries were being sent out by the Indian church to areas remote and inaccessible to missionaries from the West. The church had come full circle. Those to whom we had ministered were now ministering. There was fruit from the years of sowing the Seed.

The mango tree has sent its roots deep into the earth to find water and it will bring forth fruit in its season, even in adversity. The church is the planting of the Lord.